Borderline Personality Disorder

The Ultimate Guide to Understanding Borderline Personality Disorder and Improve Your Relationship. Stop Walking on Eggshells Trough New Techniques and Therapies

© **Copyright 2019 - All rights reserved.**

The content contained within this book may not be reproduced, duplicated or transmitted without direct written permission from the author or the publisher.

Under no circumstances will any blame or legal responsibility be held against the publisher, or author, for any damages, reparation, or monetary loss due to the information contained within this book. Either directly or indirectly.

Legal Notice:

This book is copyright protected. This book is only for personal use. You cannot amend, distribute, sell, use, quote or paraphrase any part, or the content within this book, without the consent of the author or publisher.

Disclaimer Notice:

Please note the information contained within this document is for educational and entertainment purposes only. All effort has been executed to present accurate, up to date, and reliable, complete information. No warranties of any kind are declared or implied. Readers acknowledge that the author is not engaging in the rendering of legal, financial, medical or professional advice. The content within this book has been derived from various sources. Please consult a licensed professional before attempting any techniques outlined in this book.

By reading this document, the reader agrees that under no circumstances is the author responsible for any losses, direct or indirect, which are incurred as a result of the use of information contained within this document, including, but not limited to, — errors, omissions, or inaccuracies.

Table of Contents

Introduction 1

Chapter 1 Causes and Symptoms of Borderline Personality Disorder 3

Chapter 2 When is it Diagnosed? 11

Chapter 3 Eliminate Bad Habits 27

Chapter 4 Emotional Invalidation During Childhood May Cause Borderline Personality Disorder 43

Chapter 5 Getting Help from Family and Friends 59

Chapter 6 Borderline Personality Disorder Family Guidelines 73

Chapter 7 How To Improve The Relationship 81

Chapter 8 Guided Meditation 91

Chapter 9 Myths About Borderline Disorder 107

Chapter 10 How To Speak To Someone With BPD 115

Chapter 11 Navigating BPD Cover To Cover 131

Chapter 12 Coping With People With Borderline Personality Disorder 143

Chapter 13 Alternative Treatments For Borderline Personality Disorder ... 153

Conclusion 159

Introduction

Only recently have clinical experts begun to realize the full implications of good physical health for mental health. The two elements of our health aren't really two elements, it seems, just two sides. Depression is now known to be alleviated by exercise. Our brains are, after all, just another muscle and by exercising we can increase blood flow, oxygen and release endorphins (the brain's natural happy drug) into our system.

Exercise can be daunting for those with BPD – well, for anyone – but the good news is that you don't need to join a gym and start pumping weights, at least not right away. Walking, running, cycling and swimming all offer good cardiovascular workouts to get the oxygen flowing briskly round your body. Walking at a moderate pace for twenty to thirty minutes a day is a good start. You should aim to improve your general level of fitness over a period of time and, perhaps, move on to more strenuous exercise.

It doesn't matter if you have BPD or not, walking into a gym for the first time can be a daunting prospect. With BPD you may feel "unworthy" or be intimidated easily. Physical exercise occupies your mind, however, and social sports can be good for your self-esteem. Consider joining a gym with a supportive friend or with someone else from a BPD support group. Safety is often found in numbers, even if there's only two of you!

Stress is Good for You

OK, not always, but it can be. Stress is the body's natural way to alert us to danger. Managing stress is the real trick. Some simple techniques for stress management might surprise you. Pet care, dancing and having sex are all listed as useful ways to relieve stress. Even dancing round the kitchen while you cook or clean can help you to see the lighter side of life! Singing at the top of your voice while driving works too! Joyful feelings combat stress better than any number of prescribed drugs and just remembering that however stressed you are, there are easy, simple ways to get some relief can help. However, if you begin to feel overwhelmed by stressful feelings it is important to talk to your psychiatrist and discuss the causes and possible solutions.

You are What you Eat.

Eating healthily is important and for those with BPD, taking the correct medication is also essential. Ensure you have a regular time to take any prescribed drugs each day and stick to it. Learn to cook from scratch and balance your diet so that it's healthy and appropriate for your level of physical activity. Don't forget to change your calorie and nutrition intake to reflect any new physical or sporting activities. Regular meals are important and don't skip meals at any time. Eating disorders are known to be a common feature of BPD and simply taking note of your diet, improving it if necessary, and sticking to regular meals can all help to improve your physical and mental health.

Chapter 1 Causes and Symptoms of Borderline Personality Disorder.

While seeking appropriate psychotherapy treatments is essential for those with BPD, your psychologist can't be there every hour of the day! It's likely that they will be able to advise you on local support groups or helplines where you can get additional support. In addition, simple coping skills can help to reduce the effects of BPD on a day-to-day basis. In this chapter we'll look at some simple steps and skills to help manage the condition – and particularly your emotions.

The symptoms of BPD include mood swings, self-harming, suicidal behaviors, intense emotions, emotional sensitivity and impulsive behavior. All of these symptoms have one common root – known as emotional dis-regulation. This is the ability to manage or rather not manage our emotions. As the those with BPD suffer from such strong emotions, they can be inclined to avoid them, resulting in self-harm, substance abuse or inability to deal with situations. Coping skills are designed to help limit the effects of emotional dis-regulation making managing day-to-day life much easier.

Why Learn Coping Skills?

Learning coping skills is all about replacing negative, dangerous or unhelpful ways of coping with strong emotions. BPD is characterized by strong emotion and many would argue that having strong feelings is not, in itself, a negative trait. The ways in which BPD sufferers tend to manage those emotions is where the problem is more often found. By learning new coping skills, you may be able to avoid damaging habits and ways of dealing with your emotions.

The benefits of learning new coping skills include;

Reducing the intensity of the emotions you feel.

Lessening the risk of using self-harm behaviors.

Avoiding engaging in behavior which can damage relationships.

Increase your abilities at operating under stress.

Build, or re-build, your own confidence in your abilities to deal with difficult situations.

Basic Coping Skills.

There are hundreds, possibly thousands, of different types of skills that will help you to achieve this result. However, some basic techniques include;

Support techniques; this includes finding a friend or relative to whom you can talk through issues. Support groups may also help and pair you up with someone who you can contact when the need arises.

Behavioral Activation; this is a technique designed to move the focus away from stressful or distressing thoughts for a few minutes.

Relaxation techniques. Again, there are hundreds of these and using them to simply re-focus and calm yourself is very effective.

Grounding. These exercises are designed to help you to learn to live in the moment, banishing fears, worries or distressing thoughts.

Mindfulness Meditation. This is commonly used in many illnesses which effect the emotions and is a simple technique to learn, with strong similitudes to grounding techniques.

Problem solving skills. Simple as this may seem it's an important tool for those with BPD to learn or re-learn. When faced with a problem it can become "too big" for those with BPD as a result of their emotional response. Learning new techniques to deal with problems can have a profound impact.

Some of the above skills will require input from others – finding the right support group or individual for example. However, others are relatively straightforward to implement for yourself and we'll take a closer look at them in the next few sections.

Mindfulness Meditation Skills.

Practiced as part of the Buddhist tradition for many centuries, mindfulness is now gaining increasing recognition from the medical establishment. In the UK it is prescribed as part of a treatment for those suffering from a range of emotional conditions including depression, chronic pain and anxiety disorder (to name but a few). For those with BPD it has significant advantages.

What is Mindfulness Meditation?

With many different descriptions, including that as a relaxation technique, a stress management technique or a spiritual path, perhaps the most relevant to BPD is using a particular technique to pay attention purely to the present moment without taking a judgmental approach. The last part is perhaps the most important. Mindfulness meditation techniques are varied but the aim of the technique is to experience the moment clearly, calmly and without judging yourself or others.

By clearing the mind and quietly focusing your thoughts you can achieve a calmer emotional state, thereby dealing more easily with difficult emotions or situations. Mindfulness encourages us to look, observe and experience the outer world and our own inner world. This can be the harder part of the meditation to master for those with BPD.

Basic Mindfulness Techniques.

Sit in a quiet place and take a simple object, a piece of fruit is recommended as it presents a number of sensory prompts. Examine the fruit carefully, the feel, the texture, the smell. Inhale the scent deeply, consider the shape of the object. As you do so clear your mind of other thoughts, breathing slowly and gently. After only a few seconds thoughts will begin to intrude on your meditation. They may be positive or they may be negative; either way take a mental note of them and then dismiss them. This is the crucial part of mindfulness for those with BPD. Practice this daily – at the start and end of the day are great times. Also as you develop the skill, you can use focusing in the moment at anytime, anywhere. Simply try to quiet your brain and focus on your own breathing.

Benefits of Mindfulness.

Not only can mindfulness help you to learn to banish difficult emotions, without suppressing them, it can help you to cope in difficult emotional situations. In personal relationships those with BPD often find that they react quickly, without thinking through their actions. By using mindfulness techniques, you can learn to slow that process, perhaps learning to step back, explain you cannot deal with the issue here and now as it is affecting you too strongly. This gives you the opportunity to take time and chose your behavior (and reaction) with more care.

Mindfulness techniques can be applied to all areas of your life – from driving to doing the housework. Allowing yourself to experience the moment only, and to avoid becoming overly negative, is a very positive way in which to learn how to cope with stress and strong emotion. It's important to note that you should allow negative thoughts to rise to the surface of your mind but simply accept them and move on to the next thought and the next sensation of the moment. While learning the technique some people find the example given above useful but you can focus your awareness on something as simple as breathing or as complex as a piece of music.

Self-Care Techniques.

Feelings of low self-esteem, shame, loneliness and emptiness can all be profoundly affected by poor self-care. It can be a "Catch 22" situation, with poor self-care compounding these emotions and these in turn lead to more negative behaviors. Self-care includes getting enough exercise, having good sleep habits, ensuring you eat a nutritious diet, not drinking or smoking to excess (or at all), taking any medication that you have been prescribed and managing stress well in your life. Good self-care is important for everyone but has particular importance for those with BPD. Most people will admit that when they are tired, they may experience emotions more intensely and for those with BPD this is an important factor to consider. Reducing the impact of your emotions, or the strength of them, is a helpful way in which you can learn to manage them. Here are some quick tips for learning some useful self-care techniques.

Sleep Hygiene

Reduce or avoid alcohol, caffeine and nicotine before bedtime (preferably three hours before).

Don't eat a large meal just before bedtime but consider a light snack as being either too hungry or too full can interfere with sleep.

Create a bedtime ritual and keep to it. Our brains like to respond to habits!

Use Mindfulness or another relaxation technique to help you to drift off to sleep.

Only use your bed for sleeping. Don't read, watch TV, surf the net or eat in bed. Your brain associates these activities with wakefulness. Sex is the only exception in this case!

Avoid day time napping, however tired you feel. This is important if you've had a bad night's sleep. By napping you'll continue the cycle.

Get help. Speak to your main clinician or psychiatrist if your sleep problem is chronic, as medication may be the underlying cause.

Chapter 2 When is it Diagnosed?

It is always a good idea to learn some of the things that are going to be the cause of borderline personality disorder. This can sometimes help you to determine if someone has this kind of personality disorder. But unfortunately, it is not always possible to pinpoint the exact reason that someone is dealing with the disorder. Sometimes it will be one of the reasons or another and other times it will be several of them at the same time. Plus, there is the added issue with the fact that just because a certain thing has occurred to someone or they are dealing with a particular issue that is listed here does not mean that they have borderline personality disorder.

As you can see, this is something that can be really confusing to know and understand. There is no straightforward way to determine what causes the personality disorder, but these causes can help to give a guess. Only a professional in the field will be able to go through the history of the patient, spend some time talking to them, and then determine if the causes are actually borderline personality disorder or something else.

As with many of the mental disorders that someone could have, the exact causes of this personality disorder are really complex and it has not been fully agreed upon what the exact causes are. There are some studies that show that this kind of personality disorder may be linked to post-traumatic stress disorder. This does not mean that someone has to go into war or something that critical to get this disorder, but something may have caused severe stress to the person and that may be the link to them developing it.

Most researchers will agree that often a contributing factor to the personality disorder is that something traumatic happened in the persons' childhood, but there has not been much attention given in the past to see how the causal roles of other issues, which will be discussed in this chapter, would affect the issue as well. What this means is that it is very common for people who have been diagnosed with borderline personality disorder to have had some kind of trauma during their childhood, but usually this is also going to be coupled with something else, whether genetic, psychological issues, or another thing as well.

One thing that could be causing the issues with this personality disorder are some social factors. These would include the way that people will interact during their early years when it comes to other children, their friends, and family. The child may also have something with psychological factors that get in the way of them developing the relationships that they should. These factors are usually going to include the temperament and personality which is shaped by their environment as well as any coping skills that they have learned to deal with the stresses in their lives.

What this all means is that there are a lot of different things that could be contributing to the personality disorder. No one is going to have the same beginning that gets them to dealing with this disorder, but it is important that they get the help that they need. Now let's spend some time looking at the different causes that may be to blame for the personality disorder.

Genetics

One of the main things that could be the cause of borderline personality disorder is genetics. It is estimated that at least 65 percent of the cases of this kind of personality disorder has some genes that were passed down that led them to have the disorder. What this number means is that 65 percent of the liability in the underlying disorder that is in the population can be explained by the genetic differences.

This can be a really difficult thing to understand. You may not have anyone in your family who has the disorder and it may never happen to anyone else in your family. What this means is that some of the genes in your body have made it more likely that you will develop the personality issues that come from this disorder.

The effect of the genes on this and other disorders have been done quite a bit in the past with the use of twins. While these can provide some powerful insights into the way that genes would work, it is important to remember that when it comes to twins, they are going to have a lot of the same environmental factors so they can have the same issues just because they live in the same environment rather than because of the genes. This is why it is often easier to determine what can happen if researchers are able to find twins who were separated at birth from adoption or other circumstances.

In the Netherlands, there was a study with families of twins. In this study, there were 711 sibling pairs and 561 parents and all of them were examined to identify where the genetic traits were located that would influence borderline personality disorder occurring. Researchers for this project found that the material in the genes that was associated with this personality disorder is found on the chromosome nine. Studies also concluded that about 42 percent of this variation of the disorder futures would be attributed to different genetics while the rest of it would be attributed to environmental influences.

This means that while genes can be partially to blame for the issue with this disorder, it is possible for a person to have the right genetic factors without ever developing the disorder at all. It seems that the environmental factors need to be present, as they are more crucial to the issue, in order to see the disorder develop in anyone.

Brain Abnormalities

The next thing that we will look at that may cause the disorder are issues that come in the brain. There are several studies that were done that did neuroimaging of those with this disorder.

These studies show that those who have the disorder have reductions in the regions of their brains that are in charge of the responses for emotions and stress, affect the hippocampus, and amygdala, and even the orbitofrontal cortex. There are some smaller studies that did more of this and found that some other areas of the brain that influenced the emotions that the person has.

This section will look at some of the areas of the brain that can be affected in the person who is suffering from this kind of disorder.

Hippocampus

The hippocampus is one area of the brain that tends to look smaller in those who are dealing with borderline personality disorder. This is the same area that is going to be smaller in those who are going through post-traumatic stress disorder which is why the two issues are usually linked together. However, there are also other parts of the brain that are affected, which are not affected in PTSD, which means that this cannot be the only cause of the disorder.

Amygdala

Another area of the brain that is smaller as well as more active in those who are suffering from the disorder is the amygdala. This is something that is going to be found in those who are going through obsessive compulsive disorder so this may be another thing that those with the personality disorder are dealing with as well.

There has been some studies done on this and one of them found that when someone who is dealing with this disorder is experiencing or viewing some negative emotions, they are going to have some really strong activity in their left amygdala that is not usual in most people. Since the amygdala is the area that is going to generate all of the emotions of the person, this is including all of the negative emotions, this strong activity might be the explanation of why a person with the disorder has such a long time and such intense emotions when it comes to shame, anger, sadness, and fear. This could also be the explanation for why they are so sensitive compared to the situation and how others would react as well.

Prefrontal cortex

This is an area of the brain that is going to be much less active in those who are suffering from this kind of personality disorder. This is going to be extra apparent when the person is recalling any memories of being abandoned. This little activity is going to occur in the right side on the anterior cingulate. Given the role that it has in regulating the amount of arousal that they will get in their emotions when something occurs. This inactivity may be the explanation for why it is difficult for a person with this disorder to regular their own emotions as well as the responses that they have to stress.

What this means is that because they are not getting the activity that is needed in the prefrontal cortex they are not able to keep their emotions in check and so they are going to let them go all over the place. This is one of the reasons why medication is often needed to help with this personality disorder. It allows them to get the parts of the brain working again so that they can actually start to deal with their emotions in a healthy way.

Hypothalamic, pituitary, adrenal axis

This is a long name for a part of the brain that is going to regulate the amount of cortisol that is produced. This is a chemical that is released to help the person deal with the stresses that they are feeling. Cortisol production is often going to be much higher in those who are dealing with this personality disorder, meaning that this area of the brain is really hyperactive. This is going to cause the person to experience a lot more biological stress than other people would which is an explanation for why they are more likely to get irritated over little things.

One of the reasons that this area may be more active is because it will increase the cortisol production is traumatic experiences. This is why many of those who are suffering from this kind of personality disorder are dealing with this since they dealt with some kind of trauma when they were younger. Another thing that might be causing it is their disorder is that when they have the heightened sensitivity to different stresses in their lives, the increase in the cortisol is going to make those who are already dealing with this disorder to be predisposed to experiencing childhood stresses and having them be stressful.

This increase in the cortisol production is often associated with a higher risk of the suicidal behavior that is found in people, whether they are going through this disorder or not.

Neurobiological Factors

The next issue that could be causing someone to have this kind of disorder would be neurobiological factors. These will be discussed in more details below.

Estrogen

The differences that can come during a woman's estrogen cycle can sometimes be the reason that the symptoms of this disorder are going to show up in females. There was a study done in 2003 that showed that the symptoms of borderline personality disorder in women were able to be predicted based on the levels of estrogen and how much they changed throughout the menstrual cycle. This is an effect that was still significant when the results became more controlled for the general increase in the negative effects.

The symptoms that would be experienced due to the levels of estrogen being disturbed are sometimes misdiagnosed as this kind of personality disorder though so it is important to be careful when doing this. Some of the symptoms that could go with this disorder are also going to be found just in PMS as well as PMDD so just because a woman is acting a bit moody does not mean that she has a personality disorder. Some examples of the symptoms that can be mistaken would include depression and mood swings that are severe.

In those who do have this kind of personality disorder, those who were going through psychotic episodes could be treated with some estrogen and there would be a lot of improvement. But it is important to note that this treatment is not going to be prescribed to women who have endometriosis because the estrogen is going to worsen this condition. If the estrogen is the issue with women and this disorder, any drugs that are used to stabilize the mood are not going to help. The diagnosis needs to be studied by a professional and correct diagnosed before knowing whether estrogen treatments are the right course of action or if they are safe.

Other Issues

Estrogen is not the only thing that could be causing the issue which is shown by the fact that men can also have this kind of disorder. There has been studies that show a strong correlation that occurs between child abuse and the development of this personality disorder. Many individuals who are suffering from it will be able to report that they have a history of neglect and abuse when they were a small child. Patients who have this disorder may have a higher likelihood of being sexually, physically, emotionally, or verbally abused when they were younger and this is usually abuse that has been done by a caretaker of some kind; the gender was not just male or female since it could have been either depending on the case. There is also a high rate of the person with the disorder losing a caregiver they were close to as a child and incest.

Next, those with this kind of disorder are much likely to have had a caregiver in their past, regardless of the sex, deny that they had any feelings or thoughts that were valid. These caregivers also would have failed to provide any of the protections that their child needed and often they would have neglected the physical care that was due to the child. Parents of each sex would also be reported as withdrawn from their children emotionally and may have been inconsistent with the way that they were treating the child.

In addition, the women who had this kind of disorder would report that in their past they were neglected by their female caregiver while being abused by the male caregiver and then they would experience sexual abuse by someone who was not their caregiver. Because of these findings, it is often suggested that children that are mistreated during their childhood and are dealing with issues with attachment may eventually go on to develop this kind of personality disorder.

It is important to remember though that just because a child experiences some trauma when they were a child it does not mean that they are going to automatically suffer from this kind of personality disorder. Rather, the trauma is a contributing factor, but other things are going to need to be in place. For example, the children may have been put through these horrible experiences because the parent was dealing with the disorder in their genes and then it was passed down to the child. The trauma is only going to result in the person developing this disorder if other things are present and if they are predisposed to it in the first place.

Developmental Factors

While some sufferers of this disorder are going to undergo childhood sexual abuse, this is not always a good way to determine who has or is going to develop borderline personality disorder. Often the reactivity and intensity of the person to negative emotions are going to be a better way to predict the symptoms of this disorder much better. This finding as well as the differences to the structure of the brain in these people and the issue with some patients not having any traumatic history in their path sometimes suggests that the disorder is somewhat distinct form PTSD. While they share some similarities, they are not one and the same. This is why researchers began to do some examining on different developmental causes that will affect who suffers from this disorder.

Some newer research that was published in 2013 through the University of Toronto has found that there are two patterns that can apply to brain activity that may be the underlying reason that there are issues with regulating the emotions; something that is very common with this disorder. While this goes into a lot of details about how the brain in a person with this disorder is working, it basically states that those who are dealing with the borderline personality disorder are basically set up by the brains to have emotional lives that are stormy. This does not mean that their lives are really that unproductive or unhappy, but since the different regions of the brain are over or under producing, they are going to seem like they are way more emotional than they should be.

This shows that many of the issues are in the brain. The brain is not working properly so the patient is not being fed the right kind of information or given the chance to deal with the situation or the emotions in a reasonable way. Since this is occurring, they are going to feel more intense emotions that are out of context and to them there is no negotiating to see if someone is good or bad because their brain just flips without much decision making. This is why it is so hard to treat those with this disorder; they are dealing with improper working of their brains and it can take years to get it rewired to work properly.

Other Factors

While the above factors are often the first ones that are going to be looked for when it comes to a person who is dealing with borderline personality disorder, there are a lot of other factors that will need to be taken into consideration. Some of these will be discussed a bit more below.

Executive function

While it is true that a sensitivity to rejection is high in someone who has really strong symptoms of this disorder, the executive functions of the brain appear to be the things that mediate the relationships between the two. This means that there are a group of processes that will include problem solving, attention, working memory, and planning and they may be the thing that allows rejection sensitivity to impact the symptoms of this personality disorder.

There was a study done in 2008 which found that this relationship between the symptoms of this disorder and the sensitivity the person had to rejection were much stronger when their executive function was going the opposite way and was lower. Of course, this also means that when the executive function worked at a higher rate, the symptoms would be much weaker. What this suggests is that having a higher executive function would possibly be able to help people who had a high level of symptoms with this disorder.

Also, another study done in 2012 say that when there were issues with the working memory, there might be a likelihood that the person would be more impulsive when they were also suffering from the disorder. This could explain why many people who are dealing with borderline personality disorder were so interested in being impulsive and doing other activities that they shouldn't.

Family environment

In some of the cases of borderline personality disorder, the person who is dealing with this disorder is going to have a few family environments issues that were able to cause the disorder. This is often in the form of sexual abuse. It is important to realize though that just because sexual abuse occurred does not mean that someone is going to develop this disorder and not all of the people who get this disorder will have been sexually abused. What this does mean is that there is a higher percentage of those who were sexually abused or harmed during their childhood who later develop this kind of disorder.

Often a family environment that is unstable is able to predict whether this disorder is going to develop or not. The unstable environment increases the likelihood that the person is going to suffer from the disorder while a stable environment is going to show a lower risk. One explanation for why this might be so is because the stable environment can help as a bugger against the disorder developing even if some other risk factors are present.

Thought Suppression

There was a study done in 2005 which showed that though suppression may have been a connection between the symptoms of this disorder and emotional vulnerability. Basically the though suppression is going to be the action of the person to attempt to avoid having certain thoughts even if they might be considered natural. There was also a study found later on that showed that this relationship is not necessarily mediated through this suppression, but that it could help lead to the symptoms of this disorder.

What this means is that if the person is suppressing some of the emotions that they are feeling, it could eventually lead them to this disorder. They might be holding the emotions down so deep and not know what to do with them. The more emotions they stuff down deep, the less that they are able to understand about the rest of the world and the less they will be able to properly handle the emotions that they are feeling. This can result in a lot of complexities for the person and it can make things difficult for them to figure out.

As you can see from this, there is not just one situation that is going to cause the person to suffer from borderline personality disorder. It is usually a combination of things that will get it all to start and it can sometimes be a really deep rooted issue. When you start to see the more complexities that come with the issue, you can start to understand why so much therapy and work is needed to have any hopes of doing a good job with the recovery phase, if it even get to that point.

Chapter 3 Eliminate Bad Habits

To be able to cope with a person suffering from Borderline Personality Disorder, you have to understand their various moods and actions so that you can know what to do to help them at every point in time, and so you can know how to protect yourself and prevent their actions from getting to you.

One of the biggest challenges people with this condition suffer from is mood disorder so it's very important that you learn as much as you can about mood disorders.

What is a Mood Disorder?

We all feel different emotions daily. You can wake up happy and, on your way, to work something happens that upsets you but by lunch you've already forgotten about it and you're in a good mood again.

Mood fluctuations happen to everyone but when mood fluctuations become so severe that other aspects of your life begins to suffer, especially your work life, relationships, education, and social life, then you may be suffering from a mood disorder

A mood disorder can be defined as "a serious and constant change in mood that causes disruptions to a person's life activities".

Mood disorders are characterized by alternating cycles of elevated mood known as mania or manic episodes and periods of depression. Patients will usually alternate between manic episodes and depressive episodes.

Manic Episodes

A manic episode is when the patient experiences euphoric feelings and high energy. During this phase, they are like Superman-you'd hear them talking about big projects and huge dreams. They are usually very active, happy and creative during this phase.

Although Borderline Personality Disorder patients are pretty much jolly good fellows during a manic episode, their high energy levels can also lead to hyperactivity and impulsiveness. They can indulge in habits that are harmful to them like driving recklessly, spending impulsively, having poor judgment, and overestimating their abilities due to the increased level of optimism they feel during this phase.

If you met your borderline personality disorder lover during a manic episode like I did, you'd easily fall in love with them because they are generally happy and have a positive outlook on life. They would want to go out more, take you to fun places, buy you gifts, do nice things for you and tell you that you're the best thing in the world.

They would hardly pick offence even if someone makes deliberate attempt to hurt them; however, it can come as a rude shock when some days or weeks into the relationship, you begin to see a different side of them that's irritable, quick to anger doesn't want to go out or do anything, is generally moody ad even lazy due to the lower energy levels.

What Causes Mania?

It is difficult to tell what the exact causes of mania are, but experts believe that it is caused by a malfunctioning of the brain chemicals called neurotransmitters.

Neurotransmitters are the chemicals that the brain uses to send messages from one brain cell to another, or from one organ to another.

Neurotransmitters like serotonin, noradrenaline, and dopamine are especially important for regulating moods. They basically tell the brain when to feel pleasure or went to feel unhappy.

Experts believe that patients suffering from borderline personality disorder have malfunctioning neurotransmitters. They liken it to filling your vehicle up with bad gasoline, and even though your vehicle is still running, the bad gasoline is making some parts of the vehicle to malfunction.

Malfunctioning neurotransmitters is believed to be responsible for the severe mood swings. Due to structural or genetic defects in the brain, its ability to regulate neurotransmitters become impacted so at any point in time, the brain chemicals are either too much or too little causing the patient to have intense feelings and energy levels with no middle ground.

People with mood disorders can hardly feel normal; it's either they are extremely happy and active, or extremely sad and too weak to do anything tangible.

What Triggers Manic Episodes?

Manic episodes usually take you by surprise because they often happen without prior warning, and for no particular reason.

However, there are activities that are known triggers of manic episodes. Identifying these triggers can help you prepare for when your loved one might slip into a manic episode.

Some common triggers include:

Getting too little sleep

Drinking too much caffeine

Stress

Changes in daily routine

Serious illness

Loss or death of a loved one

Alcohol or substance abuse

Jet lag from travel

Use of antidepressants drugs

Warning Signs of the Onset of a Manic Episode

Because Borderline Personality Disorder patients can sometimes engage in harmful behavior during manic episodes, it is important to look out for them during this period so as to prevent them from doing things that would harm them.

First, you have to learn how to look out for warning signs that they are about to slip into a manic episode.

There a lot of warning signs that can help you tell that they are about to slip into a manic episode so that you can be prepared.

Some of the warning signs include:

Suddenly becoming talkative

Suddenly expressing ideas that may be deemed unreasonable

Sudden short temper or irritability

A sudden surge in mood

Reckless spending

A sudden increase in optimism

How to Take Care of Your Loved One during a Manic Episode

During a manic episode, it's hard to convince your loved one to visit the hospital because this is the time when they often feel good about themselves so it's hard to convince them that feeling good is a problem.

But there are a lot of ways that you can help them manage this high energy period so that it's much more positive for them than negative, and they don't end up harming themselves.

Some of the ways that you can help them:

Calmly encouraging them to take their medications or visit a healthcare professional.

Being more observing of their spending habits and discouraging them from making investments or serious financial decisions during this period.

Encouraging them to journal: journaling can help them keep their thoughts organized, and prevent them from impulsive behaviors.

Speaking calmly to them especially when they lose their patience. They can be irritable during a manic episode too but don't try to match their irritability with equal anger. Learn how to separate their actions from their personality, and keep in mind that what they are doing at that moment is not their fault but caused by what is happening in their brains that they have no control over.

Don't raise your voice when they are raising their voice; instead, speak calmly when they raise their voice – it can help them to also calm down and reason with you. It also helps them to become less irritable.

Encourage them to work on their abandoned projects during this phase. As soon as the depressive episode sets in, there is a significant possibility that they would abandon most of the projects that they started to work on during the manic episode so it helps to encourage them to go back to these abandoned projects rather than starting another set of projects.

Encourage them to exercise. Exercise goes a long way in helping to regulate the chemicals in the brain and it can be a good way for them to utilize their high energy so that they don't have to engage in potentially dangerous activities.

Encourage them to sleep or help them manage their insomnia during this period. Lack of sleep can have severe negative consequences on a person's health so encourage them to get enough sleep. Massage therapy and herbal teas like chamomile are particularly helpful for calming the body down, and inducing sleep.

Depressive Episodes

A depressive episode is the exact opposite of the manic episode. During the depressive phase, the patient feels sad, has low energy, loses interest in things they used to be excited about, and basically withdraws into their shell.

When your loved one switches from a manic episode to a depressive episode, it can seem like you're dealing with two different people living in one body because their attitudes and behaviors are very different.

What Causes Depressive Episodes?

Depressive episodes are also caused by chemical imbalances in the brain or malfunctioning neurotransmitters that make it hard for the brain to regulate moods.

Common Triggers of a Depressive Episode

There are a few things that can trigger depressive episodes even though just like a manic episode, it often happens without warning.

Common triggers include:

Major life changes especially in their careers or relocation from one place to another.

Financial difficulties like debts or bankruptcy. Being broke can also trigger a depressive episode in patients.

Problems in their relationships like rejection, breakups, divorce or a fear of rejection.

Loneliness

Stress

Caffeine

Medications

Alcohol or drug abuse

Warning Signs of the Onset of a Depressive Phase

There are also a few warning signs that can help you tell that your loved one is about to slip into depression.

Warning signs include:

Sudden changes in sleep patterns- they may start to spend longer hours in bed.

Sudden withdrawal from society and desire to be alone

Sudden loss of interest in hobbies and things they usually enjoy

Taking much longer time to complete daily tasks

Sluggishness

Restlessness and agitation

Lack of optimism

Changes in appetite and binge-eating

Feelings of guilty

Sudden increase in irritability

Difficulty remembering issues

Reduced energy levels

When you begin to notice any of these sudden changes, you can tell that they are about to have a depressive relapse and you can start preparing for it.

How to Care for Your Loved One during a Depressive Phase

It's important to keep an eye on your loved one during this period, even more than the manic episode because thoughts of self-harm and suicide are rife during a depressive phase.

Here are a few helpful ways to care for your loved one during this phase:

Keep Track of Symptoms and Triggers: It's important to keep a track on what triggers the patient's depressive episodes as spotting the signs early can help to keep their symptoms in check.

Stay Calm: People with BPD can become difficult to relate with during depressive episodes. They can be slow to anger and irritable so it helps when you stay calm and focus on their strengths rather than their temporary weaknesses.

Encourage Breathing Exercises: Breathing exercises can help to reduce anxiety and reduce the desire for self-harm. Encourage them to take very deep breaths and count from one to ten before exhaling.

Ten reps of breathing exercise at a time can go a long way in helping a person to calm down when they are going through a depressive phase.

Plan a Lot of Outdoor Activities: This is a time when they should be out more and around other people even though they would naturally want to withdraw into their shells and be alone.

You can plan dates, fun activities, and hangouts around this period so that they can be out and around people more, and they can slip out of the depressive phase much faster.

Encourage a Healthy Diet: Depression can trigger the onset of eating disorders because BPD patients often choose food as a coping skill but the brain cells require healthy nutrients to function properly so encourage them to eat a healthy diet so that they have a better chance to snap out of the depressive episode faster.

How to Manage your loved one's Fear of Abandonment

Another important thing you have to learn how to manage when living with or dating a person who suffers from BPD is their fear or abandonment.

Yes, it's mostly baseless- you may not be planning to leave them, and you may not be able to tell why they feel this way but a fear of abandonment is almost always present in the mind of a person who has this disorder.

This fear is sometimes made worse by partners, friends or loved ones who have abandoned them in the past because of the symptoms of their illness.

If you want to help your loved one, you have to know how to manage their fear or abandonment.

Ignore Their Outrageous Actions: BPD patients have a penchant for whipping up trouble when there is none when it comes to issues of abandonment in relationships. They can come up with outrageous accusations like "Oh, why haven't you been answering your calls, are you trying to leave me?"

"Why do you have to go on that work trip with a female colleague, are you cheating on me with her?"

And in a bid to try to ensure that you're not leaving them, they can stalk you, get emotional, cry, and try to start fights or eve threaten to commit suicide.

That's just how they are wired- remember that they have a disorder that makes them respond to things differently than other regular people. So, you would have to learn how to ignore the outrageous things that they do, and recognize it as a temporary symptom of an illness because as soon as they start getting treatment and therapy, they would become better at managing their fears of abandonment.

Reassure Them Constantly: When they express their fear of abandonment, whether directly or indirectly through negative behavior, what you should do is to reassure them.

Look beyond the negative behavior.

Like when they start accusing you of cheating or trying to dump them, just take a deep breath to calm yourself, hold their hands and look into their eyes, then offer some sweet words of reassurance like "I know you think I'm going to leave you like the others, but trust me, I'm here for the long haul. Even though things are not perfect in our relationship right now, I'm ready to make it work because I love you. Please, always trust me even when you don't understand my actions, I love you and I will never do anything to hurt you".

You can say it to them or you can send it in a text or a mail- it will go a long way in allaying their fears or abandonment, and in helping them feel more relaxed about the relationship and this ultimately leads to fewer conflicts in the relationship.

Don't Play Mind Games: Most people play mind games in relationships to try to gain the upper hand but if you're with someone who has the Borderline Personality Disorder, you have to keep it straight and real in the relationship because they don't have the bandwidth to handle emotional rollercoasters or uncertainty in relationships.

Don't try to withdraw from them to make them miss you, or ignore their calls, or flaunt someone else just to make them jealous- people with BPD usually have a problem with handling mind games so just keep it straight and real with them.

Always Keep in Touch: Don't leave your BPD lover or friend for days without getting in touch. Because of their fear of abandonment, they have the need to stay connected to the people they love.

How to Manage Conflicts in the Relationship

Conflict management is another important aspect you have to pay attention to when you have a loved one who suffers from Borderline Personality Disorder.

Finger pointing and blame games would not help, what can help you get along and live peacefully with a person who suffers from this condition is learning how to relate with one another in a healthy way.

I'll share a few tips that helped me manage the constant conflicts my partner and I had, and how we were able to restore the peace and sanity in our relationship.

Don't Feed The Drama: It takes two to fight and argue. Yes, BPD patients are a pain in the neck, and they are just impossible but have you ever seen a person fighting with themselves?

For a conflict to really happen, it has to take the involvement of both parties.

It can feel unfair, like why do you have to be the bigger one but, you already know that this person has a medical challenge that is the reason why they are behaving that way so engaging with them is like pouring fire into a volcano; it doesn't help.

One tool that personally employed is humor- when my husband starts throw tantrums, I already anticipate it and I just make a joke and then we both end up laughing about it.

It will help to reduce the conflicts in your relationships if you can avoid engaging them or matching their actions when they try to start fights with you.

Don't Make Promises You Cannot Keep: We already talked about this- BPD sufferers are not too good at handling uncertainties and disappointments so it's best to avoid making promises that you can't keep to them and in circumstances where disappointments are unavoidable, take your time to explain to them. Being nonchalant about disappointments can trigger anger feats and tantrum episodes.

Set Boundaries and Establish Rules: You don't have to take everything that they throw at you; it's okay to establish rules and boundaries.

When they start 'going too far' or engaging in behaviors that are potentially harmful to you or those that are unacceptable, it's okay to calmly inform them that their behavior is unacceptable.

Take Time to Disengage: Giving each other space is also a very helpful way to deescalate conflicts. It's okay to walk away or take some time off if you feel overwhelmed.

Don't threaten to abandon them; you calmly tell them their actions are affecting you right now, and you think that both of you need some space from each other at the moment.

If you're taking time off, make sure you reassure them that you are not abandoning them but simply taking a break to help both of you cool off so you don't trigger their fears of abandonment.

Don't Force Them to Talk: After a conflict, normal people would want to talk about it, and maybe kiss and make up but for a person with BPD, they may not feel like talking immediately and forcing them to talk might just trigger another set of conflicts.

It is important to allow them to calm down and process their thoughts and feelings properly before talking about issues; otherwise, nothing they say at that moment is going to help- they'll only just make things worse.

Be Empathetic: Showing empathy can help to reduce conflicts or prevent them before they even start.

Saying kind and soothing words like "I know how you feel, I'm sorry you feel this way" before asserting your opinions or stands on issues can go a long way.

Chapter 4 Emotional Invalidation During Childhood May Cause Borderline Personality Disorder

Effective treatment for borderline personality disorder is a combination of medication and therapy. This means that finding the right therapist to work with is crucial in the success of your treatment.

Treatment with BPD will entail meeting with your therapist 1 to 3 times a week depending on the severity of the condition. Therapy is usually long-term and your therapist understands that there are no quick fixes for addressing borderline personality disorder. A good BPD therapist is one who is committed to working with you, your family and your loved ones on a long-term basis. Additionally, a good BPD therapist is someone who has the skill and expertise in Dialectical Behavior Therapy. Other treatment options you may want to consider using in conjunction with DBT include supportive counseling, forms of psychotherapy, and cognitive behavioral therapy.

When you are in the process of finding a therapist to work with, it is important that you feel comfortable around them. Otherwise it would defeat the purpose because you wouldn't open up to someone whom you feel judges you or doesn't listen. In addition it is also necessary to ask questions about their work experience such as:

How long have they been treating DBT?

What kind of training have they had?

Are they comfortable with taking phone calls outside session times?

Do they accept insurance?

How many other patients of BPD are they treating?

Before you decide on which therapist to work with, it is recommended to do a brief search of them on the internet. Most therapists have their own websites that provide information on the kind of treatment they specialize in, as well as their professional philosophy and interests.

If you can obtain recommendations for good therapists to work with based on other people's experiences, this helps to validate a therapist' skills and effectiveness in treating BPD.

Once you have decided to inquire about a therapist, visit them at their office. Observe the way they handle phone calls and inquiries because that can say a lot about a person. In fact, a good and professional therapist will even encourage you to shop around until you find one that you are completely comfortable in working with.

If you are seeking help for a loved one whom you suspect has borderline personality disorder but hasn't been diagnosed yet, be wary about using this term. The therapist may have images of someone who is engaged in self-harm or suicide and may already have an approach in mind. Your loved one can receive better treatment if the therapist approaches the first few encounters with an open mind. Even if you suspect that it is BPD, the best thing to do is to describe the traits you are observing and leaving the diagnosis to the professionals.

Choosing a therapist who is skilled with the appropriate treatment methods for borderline personality disorder is important. However, studies have shown that this counts for only 15% of the success in treating BPD. The other 85% depends on the relationship between a therapist and a client. This is especially because patients of BPD already have fear of abandonment, and trust issues.

Another important consideration in the selection of a therapist is their availability and location. Convenience and driving time should be considered especially if you or your loved one may have a severe case of BPD and emergencies may arise. Therapy will only be effective if the clients can commit to being at appointments regularly, so if location will be an obstacle you are better off choosing a therapist that is in close proximity to your home.

Financing and payment are also important, so first determine how much you are willing to pay. If you already have health insurance it is recommended to call the insurance company to find out if they cover mental health benefits, outpatient treatment, and the number of sessions covered. In the event that your insurance provider would only cover certain therapists then they may be able to provide you with the list of those approved. Keep in mind that some therapists will only accept payments out of the patient's pocket. If the therapist you choose only has this payment option available, ask if they can provide you with an official receipt that you can send to your insurance provider for reimbursement. If the cost of therapy is above your budget, you can also try negotiating for lower fees.

The ideal situation is one where your loved one as the client, and the therapist, are able to form a therapeutic alliance. This is defined as a therapist-client relationship where the therapists are able to be empathic, provide unconditional and genuine care, and helps the patient trust him/her. With this kind of a relationship the client feels safe, understood, and respected by the therapist which greatly increases the chances for a successful treatment.

Inpatient or Outpatient Treatment Center

Inpatient and outpatient treatment options vary greatly and will have different impacts. It is important to determine which treatment option will be most effective for your loved one.

Inpatient treatment, in the form of a residential Borderline Personality Disorder treatment program, is recommended for individuals whose loved ones find that everyday life with borderlines are becoming too difficult to manage. It should also be considered as an option if you feel that you don't have the time due to family or work demands to provide your loved one with the care and support that they need to get better. An inpatient residential treatment program will provide your loved one with a nurturing environment where they will be asked to participate in various group and individual therapies.

In cases of extreme borderline personality disorder, admission to a psychiatric hospital may be necessary. This is especially important in the case of a mental health crisis such as when the individual is more prone to suicide and often has thoughts of harming other people. The care provided at a psychiatric hospital is more thorough as compared to inpatient or outpatient treatment facilities since they are designed to address extreme cases of BPD.

There are two kinds of psychiatric hospitals: inpatient and partial. At an inpatient psychiatric hospital, patients are required to stay during day and night where they will be given treatment. Patient's movements are

some what limited, in fact they may not be allowed to leave their units when they first arrive. Inpatient psychiatric hospitals provide stability for people who are going through a severe mental health crisis and prevent them from committing suicide. The goal of an inpatient psychiatric hospital is to provide the patient with a stable, calm environment although hospitalization tends to last for a few months and for some, even years. But because research shows that longer hospitalizations do not necessarily mean more reductions in BPD symptoms, hospital stays for people with borderline personality disorder are now significantly shorter.

In a partial psychiatric hospital, individuals may come in treatment during the day but are not required to stay the night. This is because they are not prone to self-harm and dangerous behavior, so there is no need for medical staff to keep watch on them. Partial psychiatric hospitals help patients gradually achieve transition to their regular routine.

On the other hand, an outpatient treatment program will provide the same benefits as an inpatient program but offers more flexible schedules. It will allow your loved one to continue living and working as they need to, while receiving treatment with a set schedule of visits. It is also common for those who finish inpatient treatment programs to continue availing of outpatient treatment options as a form of support later on.

What to Expect in a Residential Treatment Facility

If you have made the decision to enter a residential treatment facility for borderline personality disorder, this is a big step towards recovery. Residential treatment facilities are excellent options in providing a healthy environment for people with BPD.

Residential treatment provides patients with full immersion towards BPD recovery. Clients are placed in their own private rooms where they are completely removed from triggers and stressors that they are normally faced with. It provides them with a chance to step back from their daily lives and focus completely on treating BPD. While not everyone who wishes to be treated for BPD can afford staying in a residential treatment facility for a long period of time, it is ideal for those who are having difficulties in managing their symptoms.

Once clients enter a residential treatment facility, they are assessed to determine exactly what their treatment needs are. Each person's case of borderline personality disorder may vary, as some people have more unique needs than others. The initial assessment is also used to check for the presence of other illnesses such as eating disorders, depression, and anxiety. Patients may be prescribed medication upon admission to immediately reduce symptoms of BPD, making them more receptive to therapy without added stress.

All therapeutic settings for patients of BPD share the same goal and that is to teach patients how to handle negative emotions, improve relationships, and enjoy better control in life. To meet these goals, clients are taught coping skills which are crucial to full recovery from borderline personality. Just like with any other new skill, these skills take time and dedication to fully comprehend. When patients put in more effort into the therapeutic process at the residential treatment facility, the faster they will be able to recover.

Residential treatment facilities will require patients to participate in regular sessions with a therapist. The combination of group and individual therapy is crucial to helping a borderline develop coping skills. Group therapy sessions also include a number of activities that can range from yoga, massage, acupuncture, and meditation.

For those who have the opportunity to stay at a residential treatment facility, there will also be chances to spend time alone and reflect on the healing process. This may be helpful for people especially those who need quiet time to think about the new life that awaits them, and how they can maximize the new life skills they are learning during treatment.

Once patients have completed their treatment, they should be committed to implementing changes in their daily lives. They also have the option of attending day treatment facilities to help them continue healing while on the road to recovery.

How to Prepare For An Appointment

If you or someone close to you is considering an appointment with a medical professional to seek help for borderline personality disorder, preparing for it ahead of time will help with diagnosis as well as treatment. Here are some things that can be done ahead of time to prepare for an appointment;

1. Create a list of the symptoms being experienced with an indication of how long they have been observed. When talking to a doctor, it is important to be as honest at all times when asked questions. Hiding things that you may not think are important because they are embarrassing can prevent you from obtaining the best course of treatment.

2. Write all your relevant personal information that may help doctors identify if you are prone to developing BPD. These include any traumatic incidents that occurred in your past or recently, major stressors in life, and family medical history.

3. It is always recommended to bring along a loved one or close friend to an appointment. The moral support can help quell anxiety, fears, or nervousness which may be an obstacle to answering doctors' questions properly.

4. If prior to the appointment, you or loved ones already have questions about borderline personality disorder it's best to jot them down. This way you can ensure that you are making the most out of your appointment.

Prognosis

If you are diagnosed with borderline personality disorder, this does not mean that you will have it for the rest of your life. Historically, mental health experts thought that being diagnosed with BPD was a life sentence. Thankfully, due to research and medical breakthroughs it is now possible to completely overcome borderline personality disorder and live a healthy, normal life again.

Most of the treatments used for BPD are proven effective in significantly reducing its symptoms.

Prognosis For Teenagers with BPD

More research is validating that the prognosis for adolescents with BPD are excellent. This is good news for parents as there are more chances that your teenager can recover completely from BPD.

Teenagers who were diagnosed as borderlines have high remission rates, with up to 85% of adolescents no longer meeting the diagnostic criteria for BPD 2 years after treatment. In fact, teens with BPD are more likely to recover and at a faster rate when compared to adults. Statistics show that 35% of adults will not meet the diagnostic criteria for borderline personality disorder after 2 years.

It is suspected that the reason why remission is so common in teenagers is because while they may show symptoms of borderline personality disorder, they don't actually have the illness. It is common for teens to exhibit the same behaviors described in those with BPD, such as mood swings, aggression, and extremely impulsive behavior. This is especially true if they are going through puberty and / or dealing with a stressful situation. However, when these environmental and biological factors are reduced, so do the symptoms.

However there are some factors that lead to a poor prognosis for BPD in teenagers. If a teenager exhibits symptoms of antisocial personality behavior before they reach 15 years of age, they are at higher risk for developing BPD later on.

How Family and Friends Can Help

Borderline personality disorder may seem like a mystery even to family and friends who want to help a loved one. It is easy to feel overwhelmed and at a loss on how you can help someone manage BPD better. But don't worry: there are proven strategies that you can use to support your loved one and even improve your overall relationship with them.

The personalities of those with BPD may exhibit mild or severe symptoms. It's usually those closest to them who can identify the extent of the illness. Living with someone who has BPD may even be described as an emotional rollercoaster, because you will have to deal with it too. Read on below to learn how to obtain treatment for them.

Create a Plan: The situation may be overwhelming in the beginning, but it's important for you to start slow. Take a deep breath, understand that everything will be alright, and that you are merely starting the process of recovery. It will not happen overnight but your patience and dedication is crucial to the success of the treatment. Start creating your plan by compiling a list of nearby Borderline Personality Treatment centers in your area. Call them and visit each one to find the treatment center that's best for your loved one's needs. While you don't have to visit them all in one day, it is best to plan your schedule so that you still have time to attend to your responsibilities.

Ask Questions: When visiting a BPD treatment center, feel free to ask all the questions you need. Whether it's a concern about the facilities, fees, or needing additional information on borderline personality disorder itself, go ahead and ask it. If early on you feel overwhelmed by all the questions you had in mind, have a list ready so that you avoid forgetting important questions.

Asking the right questions at BPD treatment centers will give you a sense of the professionalism and knowledge of the staff. It will help you make a better-informed decision on the situation as a whole and choosing the proper facilities needed, since not all BPD patients have the same needs.

Here are some topics you inquire about when visiting a BPD treatment facility:

Dialectical Behavior Therapy options

Holistic treatment options (meditation and yoga)

Treatment of co-occurring disorders

Support programs for families

Individual and group therapies

Continued support for patients after BPD treatment

Relationships With People Who Have BPD

The mere concept of relationships can cause anxiety to people who have borderline personality disorder. Relationships are successful when two people come together regardless of their opinions, quirks, and personalities. They begin when something unexplained clicks, bringing together two people who come from different walks of life.

The honeymoon stage occurs early on in the relationship, and for many these are usually considered the best days. During the honeymoon period, couples are still so in love and exert the extra effort to make the other person feel that they are loved too. Eventually, the honeymoon period will die down and people get more comfortable with one another. As the layers are stripped off, people begin to reveal their true selves to their partners. Once barriers are broken down, this paves the way for misunderstandings and oftentimes one partner may end up feeling neglected.

While relationships can be difficult for everyone, it is no surprise that people with borderline personality disorder have a pattern of broken or strained relationships. The symptoms of BPD that make relationships difficult to manage include fear of abandonment, reckless behavior, paranoia, and difficulties regulating thoughts and emotions. In order to make a relationship work, these symptoms of borderline personality disorder place added pressure on the usual challenges that people in relationships already face. In fact, individuals with BPD may resort to self-harm and suicide, substance abuse, and eating disorders which will make relationships more difficult.

If you find out that you are already in a relationship with someone who has borderline personality disorder, it is important to remember that it's not the end. If you truly love someone, you will not give up on them despite them having BPD. There is hope despite the challenges that borderline personality disorder brings in relationships but you and your partner can learn how to communicate better.

It is Dialectical Behavior Therapy that is most useful for those who are in relationships. It combines tenets of Cognitive Behavioral Therapy with elements of Buddhism to help those who are suffering from BPD. Dialectical Behavior Therapy, also referred to as DBT, teaches skills that are crucial in any relationship. These include distress tolerance, mindfulness, emotional regulation, and effectiveness in interpersonal relationships.

How To Know If Someone You Are Dating Has BPD

Dating doesn't have to be complicated, but it is clear that when a person becomes too clingy this can damage the relationship. If you are dating someone who has borderline personality disorder, you may experience clinginess in extreme cases.

However, because people with BPD are afraid of being alone, they will resort to desperate measures to stay in the relationship no matter what happens. Dating someone with BPD may mean that your partner will go to lengths in order to obtain your approval. It is very rare that they will disagree with you, since they are easily influenced by your thoughts and opinions. Individuals who have BPD have a fear of abandonment by their partner and are constantly in a state of anxiety, fear, and sadness. If you are dating someone with BPD it is necessary to understand their needs and ensure that your needs are balanced too.

Determining if the person you are dating has BPD is the first step before you change your approach to them. Warning signs to look out for include:

- Difficulty starting projects

- Needs validation from other people before making decisions

- Needs the help of other people in taking responsibility for different areas of their life

- Going to extreme lengths in order to get other people's approval and support

Chapter 5 Getting Help from Family and Friends

Living with a personality disorder like BPD can be pretty crippling and stigmatizing, given that the general public remains vastly misinformed about mental disorders and behavioral disorders.

For severe cases of BPD, it may take a while before patients can be left on their own devices again, usually requiring hospitalization and in-patient treatment. But for many cases, regular treatment and therapy can make normal life a possible prospect for individuals with BPD.

If you or someone you know has BPD, there is no reason to lose heart. Unlike many other personality disorders, BPD actually has a good prognosis for remission and a lower risk of relapse. Most diagnosed cases show significant improvement after several years of therapy and treatment, and although some symptoms may never disappear entirely, many former BPD individuals no longer meet the full criteria for BPD diagnosis.

Self-help

If you suspect that you may have BPD, there's no reason to postpone a visit to a mental health professional. Early diagnosis is crucial to prevent the onset of the worst symptoms of BPD and to treat and manage whatever symptoms you might already have.

Taking the first step towards treatment is always difficult, and you might undergo denial at first. However, remember that treatment is possible and that it is the only best option for you and your family. BPD does not need to shed a big shadow over your life.

Talk to an expert. Psychiatrists, social workers, and psychologists are the best people who can help a person with BPD. Although it might be difficult to come to terms with your condition, you need to accept it and move on to get help from people who know and understand your condition. Psychiatrists will know what to do but you need to be upfront about your symptoms and experiences.

If you want to get treatment, you need to completely disclose your symptoms to your health professional. It's also best to find a psychiatrist whom you feel comfortable with, someone you feel you can trust completely not to betray your confidence.

Once you have a treatment plan, stick with it. Your psychiatrist will help you come up with a tentative treatment plan based on your symptoms. He might prescribe a form of therapy and set regular sessions over the course of the next few weeks. Medication might also be prescribed if you find it difficult to manage some of your symptoms.

Regardless of what your treatment plan looks like, follow it to the letter. It might appear difficult at first, but it's crucial to follow the plan in order to see if it works. If it doesn't, don't despair—your psychiatrist is still feeling his way with your treatment and might make several adjustments with your treatment plan until you find something that works. Also, try to report everything you feel while undergoing treatment, and keep a journal where you can record your moods, thoughts, perceptions, and feelings regularly. Some psychiatrists also recommend taping your sessions and listening to them on your own so you can get your personal insight of your feelings and thoughts after each session.

Keep a routine. Establish a sleeping and eating pattern and routine. Moods, thoughts and perceptions may also be affected by your lifestyle and eating habits. Having a regular time for meals and getting enough sleep is one way to keep moody thoughts and negative emotions at bay.

Get some exercise. You can relieve tension, stress and anxiety in a different way by channeling your agitation in a positive way, such as exercise. It doesn't need to be rigorous, just enough to avoid the build up of stress which might turn to an emotional outburst again.

Set goals. You need to help yourself first before anything else, and if you are finding it hard to focus because of your symptoms, goal-setting can go a long way in increasing your productivity. However, make sure your goals are realistic and not impossible to achieve, and learn to take things slow especially when it comes to treatment.

Prioritize. When you set goals, plans, and tasks, try to break them down into simple ones so you won't get overwhelmed.

Foster healthy relationships. Now, more than ever, you need the help of your family and friends. The impulse might hit and you might want to drive them away, or you might be afraid that they'd abandon you because of your condition. If they truly care for you, they won't do any of that. They will still love you and give you the support you need. Stop the cycle of idealization and devaluation and learn to trust other people.

Confide. Rage, anger, and panic are all extreme emotions that strike at random for BPD patients. These negative emotions might be caused by your tendency to bottle things up. Learn to share what's troubling you with people you trust. You don't need to carry this burden alone.

Share your symptoms. In order to avoid possible triggers, try sharing your plight with other people. Don't hesitate to tell other people what and what not to do in order to avoid triggering a BPD episode.

You will get better in time. Don't expect to see immediate results from your therapy or treatment plan. Reversing the effects of BPD is a long-term endeavor, and no medication or therapy will ever cure it in an instant. Just be patient, and don't expect too much of yourself too soon. The symptoms will improve, but not immediately.

Find your comfort zone. What makes you happy? Where do you find comfort? Think about things which you enjoy, things that relax you, and people whose company you enjoy. Instead of stressing over your fears, try to let go and find ways to relax and have fun.

Join support and self-help groups. Social workers are always organizing support groups within communities for people with personality and mental disorders. There are also various online forums you can join in order to find more information and support from fellow BPD patients like you.

Find a BPD resource. There's no better way to perform self-help than to educate yourself fully about this disorder. Find out the meaning behind your symptoms and watch out for developments regarding diagnosis and treatment. Information and self-diagnosis can go a long way into making sure that your therapy and treatment plan will work.

Mythbusters

Let's get a few things straight. When people learn that someone has BPD, they tend to already have several conclusions in mind about this condition. It's not really their fault, but it's the way mass media promotes an anti-psychotic way of thinking. Often, personality and mental disorders are linked with criminal activity, among other antisocial behaviors.

So, the next time someone approaches you with some misconceptions about BPD, don't be afraid to correct them. There is a lot about BPD that has yet to be understood completely, but these myths clearly need to be stopped before they create more stigmas against individuals with BPD.

BPD individuals are just manipulative. Some people (and even some psychiatrists who don't have experience in dealing with BPD cases) have this misconception that people with BPD are just plain manipulative. For professionals, this mindset is to be avoided at all costs, especially since it won't help during treatment if you already have an outstanding bias against the patient. Besides, manipulative people don't get caught in dangerous situations the way BPD individuals do. Manipulation masters get away with crimes. People with BPD can't help themselves if they come across as manipulative. It's part of what needs to be treated in order to improve the quality of their life.

They don't really want to die when they attempt suicide. Some people think that all individuals with BPD inflict self-harm and threaten with suicide as a form of manipulation, but this is not necessarily true. In fact, living inside the head of a person with BPD can be very emotionally draining and painful, because they often feel hurt by their experiences and do seek out ways to escape their world. These means of escape, however, are often self-destructive—including suicide, and engaging in risky behaviors.

They are psychotic stalkers. Individuals who suffer from BPD are often perceived as crazy stalkers because of their tendency to cling to someone they feel close with. The midnight phone calls, constant messages and close attention they give to people they care about can give a freaky impression that they are obsessed with that person. Stalking is not a symptom of BPD, and it's a rare case that an individual with BPD becomes a stalker.

BPD patients can change, but they don't want to do it. No bigger myth could be untrue. No person, suffering from BPD or not, would ever want to be out of control of their emotions and behaviors. It's not that BPD patients don't want to change; it's just that they tend to resist change because they associate changes with emotional upheaval.

BPD patients are selfish and uncaring. Contrarily, people diagnosed with BPD are very sensitive of the people around them, and they care very much about their families and friends. Their "selfish" behaviors only manifest when they are stressed out and lash out with risky behaviors which cause harm unto themselves and their relationships to the people they love. Afterwards, however, guilt and shame usually hits home and they feel even more terrible.

BPD is caused by sexual abuse during childhood. This is often a myth associated with the tendency of some women suffering from BPD to engage in risky sexual liaisons with strangers, often coming off as promiscuous to other people. Although it's true that around 28 to 40 percent of diagnosed BPD cases are linked with sexual abuse during childhood, not all cases are at all related. In fact, the figures of sex abuse-related BPD cases are significantly lower than initial estimates by experts.

Poor parenting causes BPD in children. Not all individuals diagnosed with BPD actually came from defunct families or experienced abuse as a child. In fact, numerous cases have been recorded coming from "normal" families. There are other factors that may have caused these individuals to be innately sensitive and quick to react to negative emotions, whether perceived or real.

BPD cannot be treated. As constantly reminded throughout this book, borderline personality is treatable, although it might take some time before treatment takes effect. Some treatment options are said to be more effective than the rest, depending on a patient's most recurrent symptoms.

BPD is a lifetime disorder. This logical leap is usually upon the assumption that BPD is like other more serious psychotic disorders which cannot be fully treated and must be managed for the rest of the patient's life with medication and therapy. BPD is not schizophrenia or antisocial personality disorder; recent studies show that after 6 years following treatment, 70 percent of former BPD patients no longer meet the criteria for diagnosis.

Individuals with BPD aren't really trying. It's not a matter of trying or not when it comes to BPD. It's just that some patients may have more severe symptoms relating to emotional and thought disturbances which may be hindering effective treatment.

How can families and friends help?

Like with other personality and mental disorders, families play a crucial role in the treatment and recovery of patients with borderline personality disorder. BPD affects not only the patient, but also the people who care about him.

Experts recommend the involvement of family members during treatment of BPD. It's important especially if you can't seem to understand why the patient is behaving in a certain way. It might be confusing, and you might feel hurt especially if you've been the receiving end of a BPD sufferer's antics. Becoming actively involved in therapy can go a long way in helping improve your loved one's condition.

How to help

There are many ways you can help someone with BPD, and here are just some of them.

Make them feel that you understand what they are going through. Often, BPD patients feel confused and misunderstood. Treatment is a long and winding road and you might feel impatient if they don't show signs of development. Just try to remember, the patient is probably doing his best to respond to therapy.

Focus on the positive. Stop putting pressure on your loved one. Try to understand what he's going through and validate the feelings or emotions that you somehow understand, and then focus your attention on the positive achievements he has managed to do for this week.

Don't contradict his thoughts directly. Contradicting self-flagellating statements like "I wish I were dead," or "I'm such a terrible person," aren't really helping. It only further incenses a BPD sufferer and causes them to feel more emotionally agitated. Try stating your disagreement in a way that validates their statement, such as "I know you feel terrible about what you've done, and why you think it makes you terrible."

Give them equal attention both during treatment and after. Some patients may go on a relapse because they don't get the same attention and care they get when they undergo treatment. Give them care and affection regardless if they seem to be doing fine or if they are still struggling with treatment. Don't withdraw your affections when they get well, or that can only worsen their symptoms.

Use validation to defuse possibly explosive emotions. Instead of contradicting, acknowledge what the person is saying as something valid and understandable. Do this as long as the person's statements coincide with facts and not distorted perceptions.

Regulate your own emotions. It won't help the situation if the patient's families don't get a grip of themselves first. You need to show your loved one that you are in control, since intense emotional displays might also trigger negative emotions on the BPD patient.

Find a therapist. Finding a good therapist to work with your loved one is crucial for treatment. If there is no psychiatrist who specializes in BPD cases, look for someone who specializes in CBT or any of the forms of therapeutic treatment for BPD. You can also seek out community-based organizations and advocacy groups near your locality.

If your loved one doesn't want to seek treatment, the burden is yours to care for him and support him the best way you could. Be as supportive as you could be, but avoid reinforcing destructive behaviors. Validation and encouragement are the best things you can do to support your loved one and help him survive BPD.

Check how they are doing during therapy. If you cannot enlist for family therapy sessions, the least you could do is talk with your loved one and ask casually how he is doing in therapy. Sometimes, therapies fail because the therapist doesn't have experience with BPD, and instead of helping alleviate the symptoms, they end up getting the patient riled up during their sessions. Be honestly interested and encouraging while trying to withhold judgment on why the treatment failed.

Be humane. In the end, don't forget that you are dealing with a human being, who deserves love, compassion, and respect. No matter how those impulses seem to control him, he still needs help, and you are one of the few who can help him.

Read up. If you truly want to help out, the best you can do apart from offering support to a BPD patient is to read up and do your own research regarding this disorder. As mentioned earlier, research is still at its infancy regarding this type of personality disorder. Reading up gives insights on how best to handle the patient and how you can avoid triggering his symptoms.

Talk with his therapist. Ask for regular reports about the progress of treatment and therapy. Don't get blindsided and play a more active role about your loved one's treatment plan. If something doesn't seem to work, try out family therapy sessions so you can be more open with the patient.

Don't ignore them. When a BPD sufferer talks about self-harm or suicide, don't set it aside as an empty threat. Immediately get in touch with his therapist and report these behaviors so they can be addressed in the next session. If necessary, call the authorities to help out in case things get out of hand.

Handling suicidal behavior

One of the most dangerous complications of BPD is suicide. An estimated 30 percent of suicide attempts of people with BPD are often impulses and not really a desire to end one's life. Be wary of your response since it may be read as a reinforcement of your loved one's behavior, especially if you tend to fuss over her and shower her with attention after each suicide attempt. Here are some tips of what you could do for suicidal BPD patients and how you can handle them before you consult with a professional for a treatment plan.

First, tell the patient to not kill himself. It usually stops the impulse, as simple and weird as it may sound. Avoid dredging up old topics and issues you might have with your loved one, and focus instead at the current moment. Try talking with your loved one and ask him how he is feeling, whatever emotions he might be experiencing at the moment.

Next, try to use validation and acknowledge how he feels and what he is currently experiencing. You should probably also ask how you can possibly help in order to ease his feelings, and reassure him that you believe he can get through this current problem or crisis.

Chapter 6 Borderline Personality Disorder Family Guidelines

Are you practicing self-care? If you answered no, you are not alone, because those with borderline personality disorder often have difficulties taking good care of themselves. However, if you have BPD you need to make self-care a priority, because many symptoms become worse when you aren't taking good care of yourself and other symptoms can be reduced when you do take good care of you. You're important and you need to make sure that you make yourself important!

Defining Self-Care

Engaging in activities that promotes good mental and physical health and help relax you are the basics of self-care. Self-care activities include establishing good sleep habits, getting regular exercise, eating a nutritious diet, managing your stress, taking medications as prescribed, and attending sessions that are part of your treatment.

Self-Care is Important When You Have BPD

For the most part, those who take good care of themselves, generally have fewer physical and mental health ailments, so you can see why self-care is important to all, whether you have BPD or not. If you have BPD, self-care is even more important. That's because many borderline personality disorder symptoms are much worse if you don't participate in self-care.

For example, when you are overtired you tend to have much stronger emotional reactions or when you are stressed you are more likely to participate in impulsive behaviors. Self-care can help to reduce your impulsive behavior, mood changes, irritability and other BPD symptoms.

Making Good Sleep Hygiene a Priority

Sleep is one of the most important things you can do for yourself and yet far too many people overlook it. When you don't get enough sleep or your sleep is interrupted, your BPD symptoms can become much worse, so it's important to work at getting a good night's sleep. Let's look at what you can do.

Avoid caffeine, nicotine and alcohol - If you have trouble sleeping, you should avoid caffeine, nicotine and alcohol several hours before your bedtime.

Don't eat a large meal before bedtime - Avoid eating foods that could upset your stomach, heavy meals or large meals for at least four hours before bedtime.

Have a light snack – If you are hungry before bed make sure to eat something light, because while a heavy meal interferes with your sleep an empty stomach also does.

Create a pre-bed ritual – Establish a routine that you carry out every night before you go to bed. This should relax you and prepare your body for sleep. It might be reading quietly, listening to meditation music or having a warm bath. It's not what you do that's important, but that you do it every night at the same time.

Your bedroom should be comfortable – The environment of your bedroom should be designed for you to sleep. Things like reduced noise, lights off and a comfortable temperature are all ways to create a comfortable sleep environment.

Have a regular sleep schedule – Every day you should get up at the same time and every night you should try to go to bed at around the same time.

Use relaxation techniques – Before you go to bed, practice relaxation technique that works for you. This can include imagery, deep breathing or progressive muscle relaxation.

If you can't sleep, get out of bed - Go to bed when you are sleepy. However, if you aren't able to fall asleep you need to get out of bed. Return to your bed only when you feel sleepy.

Your bed is only for sleeping – It's not for watching television or eating or playing on your tablet. Other than sleep, sex is the only thing that should happen in your bed. By doing this you train your body that when you go to bed it's time to sleep.

No naps – Don't take a nap during the day, even if you are really tired because you will disrupt your night's sleep.

Exercise during the day – Exercise before bed should be limited because it can actually energize you and make it hard to sleep.

Talk to your doctor – If you have tried everything and sleep still eludes you, then it's time to talk to your doctor, who may be able to prescribe a sleeping pill to help you or have other techniques that might work.

Get Physical

The connection between our minds and our bodies is significant. This is why many scientists are now studying the impact of exercise on mental health, and why they are finding that exercise can have a dramatic impact on mental health.

The problem is when you are suffering from borderline personality disorder you are less likely to think about your physical health. The sedentary lifestyle is likely to result in you having additional health concerns.

There's very few illnesses that physical activity doesn't help with. Whether you walk, run, dance or go to the gym, it doesn't matter. It's not what you do that's important but that you do something. Physical activity helps a number of ways. The most obvious is that it distracts you from your current emotions.

There are all kinds of exercise regime. You can make it as simple or as complicated as you want to. Choose something you like to do, because then you are much more likely to follow through.

Make your exercise part of your daily routine. Before long you'll be looking forward to it and enjoying the benefits.

Ensure You Are Eating a Healthy Diet

If you have BPD, your feet are very important. Eating a well-balanced, nutritious meal regularly is key and you also need to avoid. Improper eating can have a major impact on your BPD symptoms and mood. Let's look at how to improve your diet.

Eat plenty of fresh fruits and vegetables

Avoid fast food, junk food and processed food

Avoid sugar

Choose lean cuts of meat

Eat plenty of fish

Reduce your salt intake

Eat regularly – do not let yourself become extremely hungry

Drink plenty of water every day

Healthy eating really isn't that difficult. It's more about making it a habit. It's so easy to grab something quick like a burger from fast food. Then we get into that habit and we spend less time creating healthy meals, which can also be put together quickly with a little practice. You'll feel much better once you are eating healthy.

Take Your Medications As Prescribed

You might not think of your medication as part of your self-care, but it actually is a very important part of your self-care. It's easy to forget to take your medication, but it is so important to take it as prescribed. By making it part of your daily routine you are more likely to remember. You might even consider scheduling a reminder into your smart phone to remind you when it's time to take your medication.

Learn To Manage Your Stress

One of the most important ways you can care for yourself is to learn how you can effectively manage your stress. Not all stress is bad. Studies have shown we are at our peak mental health when we have a small amount of stress in our lives, but not too much, stress. It is when your stress starts to overwhelm that it can be a problem and you can develop techniques to help you manage that stress. There are many ways to reduce stress. Here are just a few examples.

Play Music – Music can help to relax and de-stress you. It can create feelings of happiness and joy. It can help to reduce anxiety and it can lift you up. Best of all, it's easy to find music. Just turn on your radio or television. If you have a smart phone apps like Songza have tons of free music you can listen to.

Talk to Someone – Having someone you trust is a big help during those times when you are struggling with stress. Call someone you are close to or call a crisis line.

Quiet Time – If you are stressed make some quiet time for you. That can be a walk, a quiet relaxing bath, some time with your favorite author or anything that you enjoy. The key is that everyone must respect that this your time to unwind and you must be left alone.

Meditation - Taking some quiet time in peaceful surroundings can be very helpful when you are stressed. Find a quiet spot where you can meditate without interruption.

Grounding Exercises - Sights, smells and sensations can help you focus on the moment. For example, take a deep breath, and start to mentally list the things you see around you; listen to the sounds around you and how they change; snap a rubber band against your wrist.

Breathing Exercises - Sit somewhere that's quiet and focus your attention to your breathing. Breathe deeply, evenly and slowly letting your stomach rise and fall with each breath.

Chapter 7 How To Improve The Relationship

The first step when helping someone with BPD is accepting the diagnosis. Do not look upon it with disgust or fear. Instead, convey your full support to your loved one. This support must be clearly shown. People with borderline personality disorder are already having problems with interpersonal relationships. They do not quite know how to adjust to people, so it's best if they have emotional support.

Get the facts about the condition

After you have accepted your loved one's diagnosis or once you begin having the nagging suspicion that they have BPD, it is time to conduct some research. You should know what the symptoms are and what is myth and not fact.

BPD sufferers care

You should understand that people with BPD do care. Do not feel as if you are engaging in a one-way traffic type of relationship. Instead, understand that while BPD sufferers may display some strange or even unacceptable behaviors, they do feel remorse about what they have done after they realize what they did.

BPD is not a result of poor parenting.

BPD sufferers have been born with the sensitivity that they are displaying. Their condition is not the result of poor parenting, of having been neglected or abused. They have come with the biological predisposition to the condition.

BPD sufferers are not necessarily dangerous.

There are people who are dangerous not because they have a personality disorder. They just are. For some reason, they have the capability to harm other individuals. It just so happens that there are also individuals who have either a personality or a mental disorder who are also inclined to harm others. While it is true that some personality disorders reduce one's capability to feel sorry about what they have done, these conditions do not automatically make someone dangerous, so do not be scared of your loved one who has BPD.

BPD sufferers do not attempt suicide just to get your attention

Those who are suffering from the potentially will try to end their lives. This is not an attention-seeking act, and needs to be taken seriously. Approximately 8 to 11% of sufferers have attempted suicide.

Know how to handle their condition

With information under your belt, you should be able to handle your loved one with BPD better. Remember to use the right tone and stance when trying to get them to seek help. Do not take a combative stance when communicating with them. They likely feel alone already, so fighting with them will simply make things worse.

BPD sufferers can display all sorts of disturbing symptoms: anxiety, eating disorders, depression and even bipolar disorder. It can occur together with other personality disorders. Your loved one may act out in dangerous and inappropriate ways. They may even be hurtful, doing things that you may ordinarily assume that they are aware of being terrible. They may regret the actions later, but during the moment, they won't be able to empathize with you. Try to not take their actions or words to heart.

It takes some sacrifice to deal with someone with borderline personality disorder. You may feel like you have to protect your own mind and body from harm because you are constantly treading carefully with someone who may always see you as being at fault. A BPD sufferer also experiences extremes of emotion, from extreme giddiness to the lowest depression.

They may even try to manipulate you into doing and feeling things. So, yes, it can be grueling to live with someone with BPD. You have to prepare yourself with all the knowledge you can get so that you will not feel personally affronted each time your loved one does something you deem to be inappropriate or hurtful.

Get help

When your loved one is ready—that is, if they no longer feel threatened and betrayed—seek help for them. You may have already sought help for them even before this step. If they don't accept the reality of their condition at first, you should talk to a therapist in secret. Consult with a professional on how you can best handle the situation at home if your suffering loved one is still not receiving any form of treatment.

Encourage them to get help

To get the best help, encourage your loved one to seek stress relieving therapy. You may also seek the help of a therapist who will focus on your relationship and not just the condition itself. Many relationships have suffered because of borderline personality disorder. While you may be the understanding partner in the relationship, it is also good to be clear that you feel hurt about your loved one's behavior.

When they are focused and listening, tell them calmly about your personal feelings about the matter. You are a human with feelings. Let them recognize this and when they're ready, let them take some responsibility for their actions. It's not completely their fault but they should accept how their actions can take a toll on your emotional health, as well.

Holistic Treatment Options

There are many ways through which one can treat borderline personality disorder. It is best, however, to combine several options to help the patient recover in all the aspects of their life. Holistic healing will not only tame the symptoms but also help smooth relationships and interpersonal ties, and the patient's general ability to handle stress.

Relaxation Techniques and Meditation

With borderline personality disorder, relaxation can be a little tricky. The patient's emotions are volatile. They can change from depressed and low, to angry and risk-prone. When angry, the BPD sufferer should be treated with relaxation techniques that can alleviate the symptoms of "fight" that their brain's chemicals are arousing in them. They should then engage in activities that will relax the muscles and mind, such as meditation, deep breathing and guided imagery.

During depressed episodes, it is best to treat the BPD sufferer with massage, rhythmic exercises and yoga that will energize and stimulate the nervous system.

A combination of these relaxation techniques will help the BPD sufferer alleviate their symptoms or at least soothe them enough to make them pause for a while before engaging in risky behavior or saying hurtful things to a loved one.

Relationship Therapy

A good treatment option for those in relationships, or in a family environment is relationship therapy. Before the diagnosis was made, the non-BPD sufferer in the relationship was likely hurt by the actions of the BPD sufferer. The relationship may have been tainted by feelings of betrayal, distrust and resentment.

Through relationship therapy, the BPD sufferer will hopefully learn how to behave more appropriately towards other people. Their friends and family, on the other hand, will learn how to communicate more successfully.

Mindfulness Practice

Mindfulness is about focusing on any given moment. It sounds very simple but it is actually quite difficult to do in this day and age. Everyone is trying his or her best to multitask. Mothers have to work and watch their children at the same time. Employees in the office are expected to deliver their best work on several projects at a time. Students do not only focus on academics but also engage in sports, advanced classes, and other extracurricular activities.

With mindfulness, you literally stop and smell the roses. You breathe in the details of your world as you walk to your office building. You make time to notice the little efforts that your loved ones have made. By looking at life more closely, the BPD sufferer is able to appreciate it better. Mindfulness does not only promote better mental health, but also a better general sense of wellbeing.

Therapy

It is also good for the BPD sufferer to be treated under the guidance of a professional therapist. They will receive guidance in terms of various ways to relieve stress. They can also go through new relaxation techniques with the therapist. The sufferer will learn to understand their condition better, thus providing them with knowledge on things like: what to eat, how to deal with problems, what exercises to perform, and other seemingly simple aspects of life that they must improve to reduce the symptoms of borderline personality disorder.

Self-Care

Some commonsensical self-care habits may, in fact, help improve the BPD condition. The patient must have good sleeping habits. Too much or too little sleep can contribute to both mental and physical health issues. They must manage stress to avoid any extreme reactions. They should also eat healthy foods because a healthy wellbeing also contributes to the mental and emotional wellbeing. They should not forget or skip medications as they are there to stabilize the condition. While they may not help but be suspicious or hurt at times, they must understand that his/her friends and family are working hard to provide them with proper treatment and support.

There are various treatments out there, but they are not really cures. One of the best treatments that a BPD sufferer can have is being with understandable and committed friends and family. Through this, they will see just how loved and wanted they really are.

Can you Overcome Borderline Personality Disorder?

According to specialists, borderline personality disorder or BPD is one of the most difficult mental illnesses to overcome. After all, it does combine a lot of the symptoms that we see in various related diseases. It is a condition wherein the sufferer can find it difficult to recognize the symptoms in themselves because they're not very willing communicators.

Why is it difficult to overcome BPD? BPD is a condition that presents as a different interpretation of emotions and other people's actions. Simple misunderstandings, without the help of BPD and other personality disorders, can cause so much trouble in people's lives. So, just imagine having these misunderstandings with someone who sees the world in a completely different way.

Imagine someone who also has a different sense of self, sometimes inflated and sometimes deflated. These extremes and viewing of world as black and white can really place the sufferer in a dark place. It separates them from family and friends because there is a divide in terms of emotional interpretation. In fact, some have gone as far as calling it"emotional dyslexia".

So, you are probably wondering now if your case is hopeless. It is difficult, yes, but nothing is really impossible when you try your best to overcome it. The first step would be to admit that you need help. You must first be able to recognize the troubling symptoms of borderline personality disorder.

If you have BPD, you are more than likely functioning well enough in society. This means to say that your family and friends are the ones who are suffering from the brunt of the condition. Let it then be your motivation to get better because you want to be able to mend and maintain your most intimate relationships.

Despite the difficulties presented by BPD, it is possible to overcome the condition. There have been sufferers who have successfully improved their behaviors and attitude, thus also improving their relationships and way of living. It can be done.

However, for this to happen, you must be able to humble yourself. You must accept that people who have approached you may be right about the possibility of you having a personality disorder. It can be next to impossible for an actual sufferer to consider the fact that they need help. However, when you have finally found the strength to recognize your symptoms, you have taken the first but most important step towards getting better.

You do have to commit yourself to whatever therapy or treatment your therapist decides to put you on. For everything to be successful, you will need an understanding therapist and supportive family and friends. Do understand, though, that you have to start things.

Chapter 8 Guided Meditation

If you want the best out of your mindfulness practice, then it is worth exploring the neurobiological differences between the brain plagued by BPD, and the mindful brain. The reason you do the things you do and think and feel as you do is all in your head. All emotions are a result of brain activity, and so we need to peek beneath the hood to understand what causes your pain, suffering, and feelings of emptiness. If the reason you suffer is your brain — and it is — then your redemption from suffering is also in your brain. Al you need to do is to create a new habit of deliberately feeling joyful.

Once you understand what's going on in your mind from a scientific point of view, you'll find that it's easier to pinpoint what exactly makes you suffer. It's like dealing with pain in your stomach. You're not going to heal the pain with some antacids if what actually hurts is the bullet you were shot with that's embedded in your gut, nor will you prescribe surgery when all you need is a couple of pills to be good as new. In the same vein, we must explore what exactly is going on in your brain, so that we can find an effective, appropriate solution.

The BPD Brain

Neurobiology of behavior is the study of your brain's structure, as well as its chemistry and genetics, and how all of that affects your behavior. This field of science is concerned with the interaction between your brain cells. It studies the way your brain cells create circuitries and neural pathways, with a view to understanding the way information is processed by these pathways, and how all of this affects your behavior. It is impossible to assign all the different sorts of behaviors in BPD to one particular neurobiological cause. Before we really get into this, let's talk about the structures in the brain that you need to be familiar with, as well as basic facts about the brain.

The brain in a full-grown human weighs roughly three pounds and is connected to the spinal cord via the brain stem. The brain stem has nerve cells, also called neurons, which are in bundles.

The cerebrum is the largest part of the brain, with an outer layer known as the cerebral cortex. The cerebral cortex has nerve cells numbering about a hundred billion and is just some millimeters thick.

There are two hemispheres in the cerebrum — left and right. Each hemisphere is divided into four separate lobes: frontal, temporal, parietal, and occipital lobes. Each lobe is assigned very specific behaviors. For planning, decision-making, and coordinating your movements, you need the frontal lobe. The anterior cingulate cortex is behind the frontal lobe, and it handles your heart rate, breathing rate, and blood pressure; it's also pretty active when you're doing exercises in mindfulness like slow breathing.

The hippocampus and amygdala are both rights beneath each of your temporal lobes, deep within your brain. You have your hippocampus to thank or the different kinds of memory you have. As for the amygdala, we'll get into that in detail much later. The temporal lobe houses the region of your brain that handles sound, speech, and hearing.

Behind each hemisphere of your brain is the occipital lobe. This is where you'll find your visual cortex, which is responsible for helping you properly interpret the signals you get from your eyes.

Our focus is going to be on the two parts of the brain, which are intricately involved in BPD: the prefrontal cortex (PFC), which is the region of the brain that sits behind your forehead, and of course, the amygdala, which we will look into right now.

Your Amygdala

Shaped like an almond, this bundle of neurons is embedded deep in each of your brain's hemispheres. The amygdala is the reason you are able to process emotions. So whenever you're in a situation that causes you to react emotionally, it's your amygdala that allows you to figure out what you're feeling, and then to act based on that.

Your amygdala is infamous for handling the fight-or-flight response. As someone with BPD, your amygdala works overtime. This is why you feel things so deeply, and respond as though everything was life and death. It's why you get so upset at the little things, even when they shouldn't warrant such an outburst. Usually, when you take a step back, you can see for yourself that you overreacted, but at the moment, you feel like your reaction is completely justified. The reason for all this is your overactive amygdala.

When it comes to making memories, your amygdala is also involved — especially when said memories have strong emotions attached to them. This is a very useful role that your amygdala plays in regular situations. Say you went to the zoo, and you played with a snake you were told harmless, but then it bit you or wound itself around you tight enough to cause you pain. You feel frightened, and that memory is written in your brain so that you'll never be so willing to put yourself in such a situation again. In terms of evolution, this is good, because this is how you are kept safe and how the human race is able to thrive. As a BPD sufferer, you will find that this evolutionary defense mechanism is in overdrive. So you don't just get a simple warning. What happens is you get that memory replayed in your mind endlessly, even when the threatening situation is over. So you can see it's important that we find ways to regulate the amygdala's actions so that you're not constantly overwhelmed with "all the feels."

It's not every time that you're overcome with unchecked emotions, though. In fact, chances are you experience a lot of moments and situations in which you are just fine, emotionally speaking. It's all down to the context at the end of the day. Not everyone will get to see you at your worst. You might find that it's easier for you to get a grip on yourself when you're at work, but the second you step into your home, all bets are off. As you can probably understand, this causes a lot of confusion for the people around you, as they figure if you can get a hold of your emotions at work, then you can do it anywhere. They don't understand that it really is all down to context, and that home and work are two entirely different situations from a neurobiological standpoint.

Your Prefrontal Cortex

In each brain hemisphere, behind your forehead, lies your prefrontal cortex. That's the part of your brain that calls the shots. It's the executive in charge, so to speak. Some of its roles include:

• Deciding between right and wrong, or good and evil. It helps you weigh the pros and cons of your choices, as well as the consequences to yourself and others. Should I call in sick and skip jury duty? That means I'd be shirking my civic responsibility. On the other hand, I've really got to see what happens next on Game of Thrones.

• Helping you mediate conflicting ideas and thoughts. On the one hand, you could afford to buy another pair of shoes, but then again, you've already bought ten pairs.

• Dealing with social behavior and self-control. I really want to scratch my bum, but I'd better not. Not while I'm on this date.

Also, no, I definitely should not have sex with that random stranger smiling at me in a children's park.

- Making predictions about the future. If I don't pay my kid's school fees by tomorrow, then she's going to get kicked out of school, so I'd better forget about buying that piano and focus on paying the fees.

Now you have all the info on your brain that you need in order to understand BPD. So let's take a look at how these two structures — the amygdala and the prefrontal cortex — work together.

The PFC and the Amygdala — Team Work

Usually, the PFC keeps tabs on the amygdala, in addition to the rest of your limbic system. Here's how that looks like. Let's assume you're wearing a pair of white sneakers that cost you a fortune at your high school reunion. One of your friends who are a little too excited and hyperactive sees you and gives you a hug. In the process, he spills some cranberry juice all over your shoes. Your amygdala notices what just happens, and signals you to go Hulk on your friend. Your hippocampus chimes in as well, reminding you of all the times this particular friend has been so clumsy it cost you one thing or the other, so you get even more upset. You're about to bash his head in with a crowbar that inexplicably appears in your hands when your PFC plays the peacemaker. Your PFC helps you realize the last thing you need is to act out on your anger, because you'll hurt him, and there will be consequences that just wouldn't be worth it.

All of this happens lightning quick in your brain, and without you being consciously aware of it all. Now you know the role each part plays, you can see how it would be terrible if your PFC were damaged in any way, or unable to operate as it should. You would have a lot of trouble controlling your angry impulses. This is the reality of those who have BPD.

The Story Brain Scans Tell

Assault, vandalism, drug abuse, violence, and self-injury all fall under what is termed impulsive aggression. There happens to be ample research on impulsive aggression when it comes to BPD. One study, in particular, showed that 47 percent of pyromaniacs and vandals were diagnosed with both Borderline Personality Disorder and Antisocial Personality Disorder. Yet another study showed that the men who were guilty of domestic violence were more likely than not also dealing with BPD, compared to men who never engage in such violence.

Aggression and Your Brain

It's been found that people who are impulsively aggressive more often than not have a PFC that is a tad passive. The same goes for people with BPD, as well. This, of course, is in comparison to people who do not have BPD. The likelihood that the BPD sufferer has a dormant PFC goes up a notch when they also have to deal with PTSD.

BPD and Genes

You may find yourself wondering whether or not BPD is a matter of genes, or simply something that happens on account of the environment. To answer this question, there was a study done on Norwegians, which involved 129 non-identical pairs of twins, as well as 92 identical pairs. The scientists learned that genes could be blamed for about 69 percent of all the BPD symptoms and that the remaining 31 percent could be blamed on factors in the environment. This study closely mirrors the consensus held by most researchers that genes are 60 percent responsible for BPD symptoms, while the environment is responsible for 40 percent.

Now, I know what you're thinking: There's a 60 percent chance you're doomed. However, that is not the case. Do not assume, based on the stats; you're damned to deal with BPD for the rest of your life. The truth is with mindfulness; you'll be able to respond better to circumstances and people in your life, genes be damned. It most definitely will at least help you out with the symptoms that account for the 40 percent.

Brain Chemistry

There are three major chemicals in your brain, which have been extensively studied in the context of BPD: Opiates, serotonin, and cortisol. Let's look at each one.

Opiates: Natural Pain Killers

Whenever there is any damage to your body, internally or externally, your brain comes to your rescue by releasing opiates to help numb the pain. They are not so different from the prescription opiate painkillers you get.

It's been found that people who deal with BPD and indulge in self-harm have unnaturally low levels of these opiates, in comparison with the BPD sufferers who do not harm themselves. Ask anyone who's ever had an opiate painkiller, and they will tell you without a moment's hesitation that the drug feels amazing. It boosts feelings of wellbeing. That said, it would make sense to assume that BPD patients who self-injure are actually doing so because they want to bump up the number of opiates coursing through their systems, so they can feel better, albeit for a moment.

According to the research, if you suffer from BPD and you self-harm, then the amount of pain you feel will be nowhere near what a regular person without BPD would feel. So if someone without BPD were to attempt cutting themselves, the pain they would feel would be beyond bearable. Ironically though, BPD sufferers tend to deal with a lot of pain like muscle aches, headaches, back pain, and abdominal pain. They deal with these pains a lot more than people who don't have BPD. It is indeed quite the contradiction.

So how do we explain this? How is it that when people who have BPD cut themselves, they feel very little pain, but at the same time, they have a lot of pain syndromes? One thing to consider is that when the BPD patient cuts, it is usually during or in response to periods of complete emotional stress. In those periods of emotional Dysregulation, the ability to perceive pain drops way below normal. This means when you're not feeling stressed out emotionally, you can feel pain just like everyone else does. Yet another reason that BPD sufferers have to contend with more pain syndromes than usual is that they usually have much poorer health than the average individual.

Serotonin

When it comes to your learning, sleep, and mood regulation, serotonin is key. You can find serotonin not just in the brain, but in the digestive system as well. Serotonin levels have closely tied to such issues as anxiety, poor appetite, and depression. It's not uncommon for sufferers of anxiety and depression to experience symptoms in their stomachs. Most anxiety-prone people have to contend with a condition known as Irritable Bowel Syndrome (IBS) on account of serotonin.

Studies caused scientists to arrive at the conclusion that a lot of people dealing with BPD have abnormally low serotonin levels, and this compounds the issue of impulsive aggression. Low levels of serotonin are also highly correlated with suicidal thoughts and actual attempts.

There are several kinds of medication that all serve the function of upping your brain's serotonin levels. They are especially beneficial to people with anxiety and depression. However, I would be remiss not to mention the fact that they can have undesirable side effects. In fact, if you have too much serotonin in you, this can make you feel even more suicidal than ever before.

Cortisol: The Stress Hormone

Whenever you're stressed out, the hormone cortisol is released. It helps you completely break down carbs and proteins so you can have more oxygen and glucose in your heart, brain, and muscles. Troubles arise when you remain stressed out for a very long period of time. The cortisol builds up in your body and causes your blood pressure to rise. The sugar levels in your body rise as well, and next thing you know, your body is forced to store a lot of unhealthy fat in your stomach. As if all that weren't bad enough, your bones grow thinner and more brittle, and your body is unable to form collagen — the molecule responsible for creating connective tissue and healing your skin.

On top of all that, excess cortisol in your body causes you to age a lot faster than usual. Over time, the cells in your hippocampus begin to go down in number, which means your memory begins to suck, hard.

Now, here's the kicker: People with BPD happen to have the highest cortisol levels, compared to people without BPD. On account of these high cortisol levels, the chances of suicide are multiplied.

We've covered enough about your brain on BPD. Now let's move over to the sunny side.

Your Mindful Brain

The reason mindfulness has helped countless BPD sufferers, past and present, is because it can actually affect the parts of your brain, which we just went over. It can alter your brain's chemistry for the better. Let's see how.

A Better PFC

In the process of being mindful, you will find that your prefrontal cortex is a lot more active than it used to be. It's amazing how much the simple act of paying attention can improve your PFC.

There are various forms of mindfulness, which affect your PFC in many ways. It's not unlike the different kinds of exercises you can do, which benefit your body in a variety of ways. Consistently doing mindfulness exercises keep your brain sharp, focused, and very aware of the present moment. You will find that the brain circuitry responsible for paying attention will be better for it, and your amygdala will benefit too, as it becomes less reactive.

Yoga and Meditation

As a practice, mindfulness meditation is usually taught as simply focusing on your breath. The more you practice, the more your awareness expands. You become aware of more than just your breath, but your very presence, or self.

At the core of a lot of variants of mindfulness, there is an emphasis on the breath. The same is the case in the mindfulness, which you will encounter in DBT. This focus does wonders for you, as it increases the activity in your PFC, and helps you become better at controlling your impulses.

A popular form of mindfulness meditation is known as Transcendental Meditation (™). ; You do this twice a day for twenty minutes each time. The process involves getting your own mantra by way of the Transcendental Meditation Program. As you meditate, your eyes stay shut, and your attention is solely on the mantra you have received.

Those who practice meditation and yoga regularly often report that they feel calm, in body and mind. Studies involving electroencephalography shows the slowing of brain activity in meditators when they sit to meditate. With TM, the slowing is very easy to observe in the mid-portion of the brain, as well as the frontal lobes. The same has also been observed in yoga practitioners. As your brain slows down during TM or certain kinds of yoga, you experience less anxiety. You feel calm and at ease.

If you're not okay with TM or yoga, do not fret. It's been shown that meditative prayer, which is used by various religions all over the world, can have the same effect as transcendental meditation or yoga. I'm not just saying that. There have been studies done on Christians in the process of contemplative prayer. In one study, simply reciting the popular Psalm 23 was more than enough to increase PFC activity. In yet another study, three nuns had their brains scanned. For years, these nuns had practiced centering prayer faithfully. Centering prayer is basically focusing on prayer, or a certain Bible verse, with the point being to experience oneness with God. The brain scans of the nuns before and after the prayer showed a remarkable difference. During the prayer, there was an increase in blood flow to the prefrontal cortex — significantly more than when they were not praying.

In Zen Buddhism, you have a practice known as Zazen. This is also called the "sitting meditation." There are actual Zazen retreats where, for days, you don't say a word, and you remain sitting for as long as sixteen hours each day. You could try this, but please don't try to take on too much too fast. All you need is 10 to 20 minutes each day for you to reap the benefits. To do Zazen, all you need is to sit down, cross-legged on a comfortable cushion. Place your hands upon your laps, and leave them there. Your eyes must remain open for this one. Your gaze will be focused several feet ahead of you, downwards. The usual thing to focus on would be a Buddhist lesson, but since chances are you aren't a Buddhist, you can simply keep your attention on your inhales and exhales. Do this consistently, and you will reap amazing results.

How Mindfulness Affects Your BPD Brain

As I mentioned earlier, mindfulness has become an indispensable component of modern-day psychotherapy, especially when it comes to Dialectical Behavioral Therapy (DBT), Mindfulness-Based Cognitive Therapy (MBCT), and Mindfulness-Based Stress Reduction (MBSR). That said, there sadly is not enough research on using mindfulness by itself as a way to treat BPD. There has only been one study so far, by Sauer and Baer, published in 2011.

In this study, there were 40 people with BPD. They were all told to write about times when they had gotten exceptionally angry. They only had to write for ten minutes and then stop. When they were done, the researchers took a look at the effects of focused and mindful attention for the short-term, to see how they handled the stress of thoughts about why people treated them poorly. Next, each of the participants was randomly assigned to either continue to think about such thoughts about why people treated them that way, or to simply be mindful and self-focused for some time. Next, they were given a task to see how well they would handle distress. The group who were mindful were able to handle the distress a lot better than those who were focused on their anger, and also stated that they felt a lot less angry after the meditation period.

If anything, this single experiment shows that you can indeed experience significant benefits from deliberately practicing mindfulness. Don't be dismayed about the fact that there is just one study. The fact is that there are myriads of studies that have been conducted on the use of mindfulness in conjunction with other treatment modalities to help people who have BPD, and in each of these studies, the proof is irrefutable that mindfulness multiplies the beneficial effects greatly.

Chapter 9 Myths About Borderline Disorder

Myth 1: Borderline Personality Disorder Is Not Treatable

This is not true. BPD is a condition that is treatable. If you or your loved one has BPD, it is important that you seek professional help for treatment. One thing you need to bear in mind is that having a diagnosis does not mean that you will experience the symptoms to eternity. You must be willing to seek effective treatment to greatly lower the severity of your symptoms so that you can enjoy living a perfectly normal life.

On the other hand, what you need to note is that even without treatment, the symptoms will gradually ebb and flow as time goes by. In fact, there are people with BPD who are able to function at a higher degree compared to others, making the recovery process different for each person.

Myth 2: All People with BPD Are Victims of Childhood Abuse

Too often, people who mean well or are very close to us do not really understand BPD. They tend to believe that it is caused by past experiences of abuse during childhood. Because of this kind of belief, the manner in which you interact with the people around you change. It also affects how you talk to people –

something that is frustrating especially if you have no history of abuse.

While there are people with BPD who are victims of abuse and neglect, generalizing the cause of the disorder might feel as though people do not understand you. in fact, you may start to feel that you are different from the rest – in a negative way. This means that each one of us must view BPD with an open mind.

As we have mentioned previously, there is no specific cause of BPD yet. However, the cause is perceived as a combination of both environmental and biological factors.

Myth 3: Children and Adolescents Cannot Be Diagnosed With BPD

As we have already mentioned, adolescents and children can be diagnosed with BPD. However, based on the general beliefs that personality is still under development among teenagers, diagnosing children and teens is something that has been controversial for a very long time.

According to the Diagnostic Statistical Manual (DSM-V), there are clear standards that define what BPD is during the process of diagnosis. This means that when this disorder is being diagnosed, a lot of care must be exercised as this may be confused with typical adolescent behaviors. The best way is to seek help from a professional therapist with experience with BPD so that they can accurately distinguish them. With an early diagnosis, you will be able to get the right intervention for you to start your recovery journey.

Myth 4: Is a form of PTSD or mood disorder

Well, what is important to note is that BPD is very different from PTSD or any other form of mood disorder. Despite the fact that BPD symptoms are somewhat similar to those exhibited by someone with PTSD or Bipolar disorder, the truth is that they are very distinct from each other.

Additionally, based on the fact that most healthcare providers lack knowledge and insight about BPD, there is usually a high chance for misdiagnosis that adds on to the confusion. In fact, the medications that are used in PTSD are very different from those used in the treatment of BPD. Therefore, when you work with a therapist with a background knowledge and experience with BPD, you will be able to get an accurate diagnosis and an effective treatment plan.

Myth 5: BPD Is Only Found in Women

Most people think that BPD is gender sensitive. Well, the truth is that it affects both genders. However, according to one study, this disorder is more prevalent in women compared to their male counterparts. In fact, it is shown that the disorder occurs at least 2-3 times more frequently in women than in their male counterparts. What is interesting is that recent studies have reported an equal prevalence in men and women.

Don't get me wrong, this does not in any way mean that women are highly likely to develop BPD. It only means that the symptoms men discuss are not accurately linked to the disorder – depression, post-traumatic stress among others. In other words, the hallmark of BPD is instability as well as poor control of impulses – something that affects both genders equally.

It is important of note that this myth is accompanied two harms. First, it increases the stigma associated with the disorder in women eventually contributing to women being less receptive to the diagnosis. Second, it contributes to the decreased awareness of the disorder in men. Because of this, there will be missed diagnosis among men, ultimately leading to inadequate treatment and continued struggles.

Myth 6: If You Know One Person With BPD, You Know Them All

One thing that you must note is that we are all unique beings, even if you are someone's twin. Having BPD does not change this fact.

According to the DSM-v, there are specific criteria that must be met for one to be said to have BPD. This criterion includes an impaired personality functioning as well as impaired interpersonal relationships. However, of importance to note is that the manner in which these symptoms manifest varies from one individual to the next.

Additionally, not all individuals experience specific symptoms the same way. In other words, what someone considers challenging in a relationship may not be the same as what the other considers difficult. Therefore, your experience of BPD does not have to be the same as what another person experiences – we are unique beings with unique experiences.

Myth 7: Is not a valid psychiatric diagnosis

Looking back into its history, what is interesting is that several mental health professionals did not agree that borderline disorders is a valid diagnosis. Because of this lack of agreement, there was increased confusion on what the distinguishing symptoms of the disorder are. However, with improved research, this disorder was included for the very first time in the third edition of Diagnostic and Statistical Manual (DSM-III) in 1980.

Since then, the support for a specific name used in the diagnosis of BPD has significantly increased. This is mainly the reason why the disorder has been shown to have significant association with specific biological disturbances in the brain. The genetic factors are the reason why there is a significant risk of people developing this disorder.

Additionally, it is important to note that the medications that are aimed at reducing the core symptoms of the disorder modulate the activity at specific receptor sites in some neural pathways, hence demonstrating the above biological disturbances.

Despite all these facts, there is still agreements on what the specific name of BPD should be. There are researchers who have emphasized on the emotional disturbances associated with the disorder stating that it should reflect that as well. There are others who believe that the name should reflect more on though disturbances, impulsivity and relationship impairment. It is this increase in complexity of the symptoms and the difficulty in making an accurate diagnosis that happens mainly when this is handled by a clinician that is not experienced.

Ultimately, this kind of myth is very harmful since it causes so many people with the disorder to be misdiagnosed. Realize that, in medicine, one of the greatest stigmas is that associated with an inaccurate diagnosis. The most common misdiagnosis in BPD includes; bipolar disorder, anxiety and panic disorder, depression, PTSD and ADHD among others.

Unfortunately, this kind of misdiagnosis is accompanied by several years of ineffective treatment and an increased frustration on the patient's part and their families. It also lowers their hope for the future. That said, there are increased events happening in the field indicating that this general situation is currently under the process of change for the betterment of those with the disorder and their families.

Myth 8: BPD does not respond well to treatment

One thing you need to note is that this kind of myth can be very harmful. This is because it greatly discourages patients and their families from seeking early help. Because of this, there is continued suffering, lack on hope in the future, disruption of social, work and educational activities.

Unless there are specific modifications made in the psychotherapeutic treatment approach of the disorder, patients with BPD will rarely improve and others becoming even worse.

Even with the use of psychotherapeutic approaches, a large number of patients with BPD still fail to show sustained improvement. This is something that seemed especially true for those with moderate to severe forms of the disorder. However, today, there is reliable research that demonstrate evidence of patients with severe BPD having significant improvements with the right treatment.

Apparently, the most effective therapeutic approach for most patients with BPD is a combination of psychotherapy and medication. However, this is not really applicable for those with mild forms of the disorder. The mild forms often respond well to psychotherapy alone.

Myth 9: Medications have limited use in treatment of BPD

It is this kind of myth that mostly interferes with BPD patients receiving an effective form of treatment that would result in prompt, sustained and substantial improvements. This myth appears to be based on the conviction that the main cause of BPD is environmental factors – at least partly.

Logically, the primary treatment in such a case would be the use of psychotherapy with the main aim of reversing the psychological outcomes of early trauma. Additionally, it has been proposed that medications often interfere with the psychotherapy process mainly because they offer patients with unrealistic hope of a quick recovery instead of improvement based on sustained and hard task of psychotherapy.

Based on clinical experience, there is evidence that shows that medications alone significantly lower the number of core symptoms of BPD. This is especially true for those with moderate to severe cases of the disorder. Seemingly, this kind of reduction allows patients with the disorder to effectively engage in psychotherapy contributing to a greater and fast improvement.

Chapter 10 How To Speak To Someone With BPD

In general, people with BPD do not want special treatment. They just wished to be loved; an emotion which, thanks to traumatic upbringings, they may never have truly experienced. For BPDs simple things such as maintain friendships or cohabiting can be enormous challenges.

People with BPD exhibit heightened levels of sensitivity, meaning even the smallest criticism can cause great offense, leading them behave with aggression and hostility. In addition, they are prone to misconstruing things that are said to them and taking offense when none was intended.

These factors can make relating to someone with borderline personality disorder a complete minefield. While you want to treat your loved one the same way you would others, you must also be aware of the erratic behavior their disorder can cause.

Here are few ways to speak to and relate to a friend, partner or family member suffering from BPD:

What to Do:

Ensure your meaning is as clear as possible. Do not rely on subtleties or facial expressions to get your meaning across.

- Offer ongoing and regular support. Listen to them, offer assistance and comfort when needed.

- Validate what they are going through. Acknowledge that, while you may not be able to relate to their experience, you understand it is very real to them.

- If you understand the way they are feeling, tell them. But if their feelings do not make sense to you, try to find out more. Ask questions. Let them know you really want to understand. Encourage them to tell you more about the things they are feeling and why.

- Give them hope by acknowledging that other sufferers of BPD have gone on to live long and happy lives.

- Acknowledge that the person is suffering and help them break their goals down into small, manageable steps.

- Have realistic expectations. The nature of BPD means setbacks are commonplace. Do your best to remain positive and encourage the person to do the same.

- If it is appropriate, ask them about their BPD management plan and find out what role you can play in implementing this.

- Communicate your boundaries clearly. Tell them what you are not prepared to accept, be it abusive language, violence, threats etc.

- If they are agitated, do your best to respond in a calm manner. If you feel in danger, remove yourself from the situation and call for help.

- Listening and reflecting on what you have been told is perhaps the most effective way of communicating with someone with BPD. Even though you may disagree with every word that comes out of your loved one's mouth, acknowledge that listening is not the same as agreeing to someone. You are simply accepting the person's emotions and perspective.

- Ask open-ended questions that encourages your loved one to share pieces of their life, such as "Tell me what happened today to make you feel like this?" or "How is your week going?"

- Summarizing back what you have been told. This helps someone with BPD feel heard and valued. For example, if your partner shares that she thinks you don't love her as much as you used to, you could say, "All right, you feel that I don't love you as much as I used to." Again, by doing this, you are not agreeing with the statement, you are simply acknowledging the emotions and perspective of the other person. Avoid the temptation to point out all the flaws in the argument remind yourself that the goal of this reflection is not necessarily to agree. It is not about proving who is right or wrong. It is about helping someone you love to feel valued and heard, and about deescalating conflict before it transmutes into a crisis.

- Focus on emotions, not words. BPD sufferers are prone to speaking in ways that may come across as hurtful or antagonistic, and it can be difficult not to focus on these words. But rather than pulling your loved one up on something they may have said, look beneath their words to the core emotion beneath. If you sense your loved one is struggling, ask questions such as: "It seems as though you are feeling hurt right now, is that right?" Asking questions such as these will validate your loved one and their feelings and help them feel as though they are being heard.

What Not to Do:

- Do not attempt to take control of the person's life. Allow them to make their own choices and simply offer your support. Do not let this become a source of conflict.

- Avoid being drawn into their conflicts with other people. Do not be drawn into their attempts to do so.

- Do not try and talk them out of their feelings. A BPD sufferer might come to you with a claim like "I am a terrible person." Flat out disagreeing with this with a comment like: "You're not a terrible person," has the effect of invalidating their thoughts and feelings. Instead, try to understand what it is that has made them feel this way. Ask questions and listen carefully. Find out if there was something specific they did to make them feel like a terrible person. From there, engage in practical problem solving – ask them what they can do to rectify the situation. Doing so gives the BPD sufferer a sense of being in control of their own lives and emotions.

- Do not attempt to be their therapist. Instead, assist your loved one in finding the right healthcare professional for them and offer your support throughout their treatment.

- Do not get defensive. While it can be challenging not to take accusations and criticisms personally, acknowledge that it is not about you. This is just a manifestation of the BPD. Remind yourself of this on a regular basis and do your best to see beyond the illness to the person you love beneath.

How to Communicate effectively during a crisis

When a loved one is in the midst of a BPD episode, they may become aggressive, insult you or hurl out unfair accusations. As human, our natural response is to become defensive and counter their arguments with hostility and aggression of our own. But when dealing with a BPD sufferer, acting such a way will only exacerbate the situation. It is important to remember that someone with BPD finds it difficult to see things from someone else's perspective. They have difficulty telling the difference between a minor issue and a full blown catastrophe. When you behave defensively, they see this as a sign that they are not valued. This will lead them to believe that you do not want to be around them, triggering their deep-seated fear of abandonment. This then leads them to act recklessly or in a self-harming manner.

Instead, when your loved ones become reactive, take time to pay attention to what they are saying, without pointing out the holes in their argument. While it is easier said than done, do your best not to take their attack personally. After all, it is not about you. If your loved one makes a point about something you did wrong, or something you could improve on in the future, acknowledge and accept their point, make your apology, and attempt to discuss ways you can improve in the future. When someone with BPD feels as though they are being heard and taken seriously, the situation is less likely to get out of hand. If, however if the conflict increases to points of threats, aggression or a tantrum, it will be most beneficial to walk away and attempt the conversation again when they have calmed down.

How to Identify an Emergency

While disparaging self-talk is a common feature of borderline personality disorder, particular among those suffering from 'quiet' BPD, the sad reality is self-harming and suicide is all too common among people suffering from this disorder. When you are around a person with BPD, it is important to be vigilant and aware of any attempts at self-harming that may be taking place. When someone with BPD is reactive, it can easily escalate to the point where they will consider self-harming. It is important, however, not to plant the idea of self-injury or suicide in their head by outwardly asking them if they are considering it. Instead, provide a space where they can speak openly about what it is they are feeling or experiencing. This will then allow you to make a decision about whether to seek professional help on that occasion.

Be aware that there are several subtle signs that may indicate a person is considering suicide or engaging in self-harm. These include shaving off their hair, isolating themselves from others, excessive scratching or a reduced appetite. These less overt symptoms represent the BPD sufferer's inability to discuss their emotions outwardly. Being alert to these symptoms and seeking help accordingly can stop a crisis from escalating and requiring serious psychiatric or medical attention.

All suicide and self-harming attempts should be taken seriously. Even if they are done to seek attention, they are still indicative of deep emotional trauma. While it is important to get your loved one professional assistance in any situation involving self-harm and suicide, seek help immediately if any of the following occurs:

- The person has deliberately injured themselves.
- The person is expressing suicidal thoughts or talking about killing someone else
- The person is acting in an aggressive and abusive manner
- The person has become disoriented; i.e. they do not know who they are, where they are, or what day it is.
- The person has become delusional or is having hallucinations
- The person has become severely affected by drugs and/or alcohol and is acting in a reckless manner.

If you don't believe the situation has escalated to the point of being life threatening, however, refraining from calling the emergency services. Doing so every time your loved one speaks of hurting themselves will signal to them that they have a great amount of power over you and that by threatening to self-harm, they can effectively put an end to any conflict or argument. Instead, when your loved one speaks about self-harming, ask them what they would like to do about the situation. Suggest calling their therapist or an emergency hotline or going together to the emergency room. Doing this gives the BPD sufferer back an element of control, which can assist in calming their runaway emotions.

What to Do When You Feel Overwhelmed

There is no doubting that having a loved one with BPD is a struggle. There are bound to be times when you feel overwhelmed and unable to cope. This is exacerbated by the fact that the person you love with BPD will generally be unable to fulfill the supportive role of parent, friend of partner, that they otherwise would.

Because of this, it is crucial to have a strong network around you of people you can rely on in times of exhaustion, stress and overwhelm. Allow yourself plenty of time to engage in hobbies and relaxation activities with friends who you can be open with. Ensure too that you have people you can speak openly to about the experience of living with someone with borderline personality disorder. This may be a therapist or other health professional, a support group, GP or religious leader.

Involving other people in your support and care of the BPD sufferer can also be invaluable. Caring for someone with a mental illness should never fall to one person alone. Ensure there are a number of people around you who are well-versed in dealing with the individual with BPD and are able to act calmly and rationally in times of crisis. The more people around the BPD sufferer who know effective strategies for dealing with their reactivity, the less likely it is that a crisis will occur. Depending on the situation, your loved one's friends, siblings, parents, children or extended family members are all people who can be turned to for support.

Manage your expectations with regards to recovery

When dealing with a physical illness, recovery is often very black and white. But recovery is completely different when it comes to mental illness. Vary rarely does recovery see the complete elimination of symptoms and it is unlikely that someone suffering from a mental health disorder will ever be able to completely dispense with the need for therapy, medication or other treatments. When dealing with borderline personality disorder, recovery can be measured in a number of ways.

A sufferer in recovery will experience less frequent emotional outbursts, and these outbursts will decrease in intensity. There will be less incidences of self-harming and other impulsive, reckless behaviour. While it is of course possible that there will be relapses, such crises will likely be resolved much more quickly than in the past. As their symptoms improve, your loved one will likely feel more and more confident taking steps towards living a full and successful life. Offering your support at every step of the journey will go a long way towards assisting this recovery.

Being in a Relationship with Someone with BPD

ften, people with BPD are very charismatic and energetic, so it is not difficult to be drawn to them. For this reason, many people find themselves in relationships with sufferers of borderline personality disorder. But the challenges of this illness mean a relationship with such a person is likely to be a cycle of perpetual arguments and dramas.

But while conducting a relationship with someone with BPD can be a challenge, if you have found a partner whom you love and care for, the relationship is likely worth pursuing. The key lies in knowing what to expect, and how your partner's disorder may manifest itself.

Understanding Your Partner

To really understand what is going on inside your partner's head, ensure you have read Part One of this book; a detailed overview of borderline personality disorder, its causes and the ways it can manifest. But here are a few of the traits of BPD that can be most prominent within a romantic relationship.

As people with BPD have such difficulty controlling their emotions, they often react with intense joy and gratitude if their partner does even the smallest kind thing for them. The flip side of this is that criticizing a partner with BPD can result in intense anger and hurt. As we have learned, people who suffer from BPD can be very sensitive to the way others treat them and even the smallest criticism can cause them immense amounts of hurt. Sufferers of BPD will experience often violent mood swings, which can be difficult to anticipate. Recognize that this is a symptom of the disorder, and likely not directly related to something you may or may not have done.

Sufferers of BPD fear abandonment and rejection, and this is never more heightened than in a romantic relationship. Experiencing even the smallest amount of conflict can lead your partner to believe that you are about to leave them. Sometimes, in order to avoid this rejection, they will pre-emptively end the relationship in order to be the one to do the "abandoning." Sufferers of BPD will have to work harder than normal to allow themselves to trust their partner and believe that they are not going to leave them.

You have probably noticed your partner tends to pick fights with you when things seem to be going well. People with BPD have often grown up surrounded by such trauma that peace and harmony in a relationship is completely foreign. In order to regain a sense of normalcy, they will seek to uproot this security through aggression, hostility and other damaging behavior. Peace and harmony can actually leave someone with BPD feeling empty and numb. In order to make themselves feel alive, they may attack you, or create conflict in another way. This helps them feel something, which, in their eyes, is better than feeling empty.

In addition, the BPD sufferer's propensity towards black and white thinking means they will often see you as either all good or all bad, often alternating rapidly between intense love and admiration to a crushing dislike and disappointment.

How to Cope

The unpredictability of being a relationship with someone with BPD can cause you to have doubts of your own. It may feel as though the more you love your partner, the less they seem to love you. All this conflict and confusion may have you doubting whether you have the strength to maintain the relationship. These concerns can be heightened by the fact that you don't have your partner to rely on or confide in. This can leave you feeling lost and alone. Implementing the following solutions can make living with BPD much more manageable:

- Get information. Learn as much as you can about what it is like to suffer from BPD. This will help increase empathy in the relationship, and help you understand the struggles faced by your partner on a daily basis. By familiarizing yourself with the traits of the disorder, it should become clear to you that your partner's challenging behavior is the result of an illness, rather than a choice.

- See a counsellor. Seeking support from a mental health professional can be invaluable to both sufferers of BPD and their loved ones. You may choose to attend therapy sessions alone or as a couple.

- Communicate. Communication is vital in any relationship, but when a partner suffers from BPD, learning how to effectively communicate is of utmost importance. It is crucial however that you take care not to say anything that your partner may perceive as a slight, or may make them feel unloved, or as though the relationship is about to end. Ensure that all discussions you have come from a place of love, rather than attacking your partner or seeking to put them down.

- Ensure your meaning is clear. BPD can cause sufferers to misconstrue what others are saying to them. For this reason, it is important to make sure you communicate your meaning as effectively as possible. Do not assume your facial expression is enough to convey what you are thinking.

- Hold discussions only when your partner is calm. Avoid raising important issues with your partner when they are suffering from an episode of BPD, such as exhibiting mood swings. When faced with decision-making in such a state, a BPD sufferer is likely to act rashly, without thinking the issues through. They are also more likely to be defensive or aggressive and may turn to self-deprecating or self-harming behaviors in order to help them cope.

- Offer support. We all need support from our loved ones from time to time, and BPD sufferers are no different. Make sure your partner knows you are there for them, in good times and bad.

- Foster a sense of independence in your partner. As we know, BPD can lead a person to greatly fear rejection. Even the smallest of separations such as a vacation or work trip can be a source of immense stress. But these separations can be beneficial for fostering a sense of independence in your partner. Make sure you have parts of your lives that are independent from each other; your own hobbies and circles of friends. While of course it is wonderful to have a partner with whom you can share so much of your life, having separate interests is great for your partner's sense of independence. If you are apart for longer than a few hours, it can be helpful to check in on your partner, to ensure they understand that the separation is only temporary and that they are not being rejected.

- Avoid blaming everything on their mental illness. Remember that your partner's BPD does not define them. Avoid linking every part of their behavior to the BPD. After all, it is just one facet of who they are.

Doing so can cause the disorder to become something of a put-down. See past the illness to your partner's personality and avoid labeling.

- Take threats of self-harm seriously. Threats of self-injury or suicide should always be taken seriously with a partner suffering from BPD. If your partner begins to exhibit signs of self-harming or suicidal behavior, call their therapist or your local suicide prevention helpline.

- Practice self-care. Living with a partner with BPD can be an enormous challenge. It is important to allow yourself time to step back and relax. Ensure you have your own support network in place; people you can rely on if the stress becomes overwhelming. Prioritize time for friends and hobbies, both alone and with your partner.

Chapter 11 Navigating BPD Cover To Cover

The HOW We Do It

This process is represented by the following essential key aspects: honesty, open-mindedness, and willingness. I learned the importance of these three necessary ingredients from the Alcoholics Anonymous program, and like most recipes, if you leave one of these ingredients out, the results will not be good.

Honesty

If you are not honest to and with yourself first, you will always have problems not being able to trust yourself – and if you can't trust yourself, you won't have any quality of life, no matter what else you do regarding efforts made at self-improvement or development. I now call bull on myself and on anyone else who is still using the same old "stinking thinking" on that one.

If you are not honest with people in your life, including being dishonest by omission (my old favorite excuse as to why it was okay to not be 100 percent truthful – they didn't ask, so I did not feel I had to tell), then you are not to be trusted at all. And if you can't be trusted, what kind of friend are you or will you be?

Openminded

When we allow ourselves to be open to the possibilities, then truly incredible things can and will come into our lives. But, if we are not open, just as certainly, they can't and won't. That is a fact.

Willingness

Are you willing to be willing? It is easier said than done, but thankfully, to be willing is really a state of mind – one determined by you. If you are willing to go to any lengths to recover your life and learn how to manage your mind, I can promise that you will be living a life that you only dreamt was possible. However, if you aren't willing to be willing, then you will have to be willing to settle for what you have had in the past. I believe that since you are still reading this book, you have decided you are willing to be willing. And that is amazing.

One tough question for you is this: are you willing to accept the fact that as part of your growth, you will have to become willing to sit with being uncomfortable? You must be willing to sit in your uncomfortable feelings, uncomfortable silences, and uncomfortable periods, and you learn through them that it becomes the way for you to be comfortable with your feelings, emotions, and not needing to speak. You will get a feeling of comfort in your skin and within yourself – for some of us – for the first time ever. And so, I am willing to be willing, as I know the cost if I am not and the rewards if I am.

Willing to be Uncomfortable

A few weeks into working with Olivia during a particularly difficult conversation, I had to literally put my hands up in a T for the universal time out sign to have her cease talking. She would ask me a question, and before I would get to the third word in my response, she would launch into a tirade about why she felt justified in wanting me to answer her question the way she wanted. Well, I figured it wasn't a good use of either of our time or energy, and I was assertive the next time she did the same thing. She didn't like it and got quite frustrated with me. She proceeded to tell me, in a very defensive tone of voice, "I don't think that it's a good idea for us to continue talking about this. You obviously don't understand how I feel, and what I went through."

Although I did understand, I simply nodded my agreement to let her know that I heard and said nothing else. We both remained quiet for the next few minutes, and I could see her facial expressions changing, as though she was expecting me to resume the conversation and defend my position. When I didn't, she eventually looked up sheepishly and apologized for not allowing me to talk. Simply by refusing to engage with her and giving her a couple of minutes of sitting in an uncomfortable silence, she realized that it really was a one-sided conversation. At that point, we both had a little giggle and talked about it a bit further before concluding the session.

Financially, Olivia had been struggling with working part-time serving while attending university distance learning to earn her social work degree. So, even though the effort of getting up and putting one foot in front of the other every day is huge, Olivia draws her strength from her love for her daughter, Rosie, first, and then from her desire to change her life and get well. She has a willingness to do whatever it takes to learn how to manage her mind and her life to conquer BPD and be able to have a life she loves living. She has told me that she is already noticing positive changes in her thinking and in her behaviour since incorporating FORDitude into her life. Rosie is also benefiting from Olivia's improved mental health and overall well-being. Together they are more engaged in living a healthier lifestyle, which includes meal planning and fun with food purchases and preparation, a water drinking chart on their fridge complete with stars and hearts, a more consistent sleep schedule that benefits both mom and daughter, daily activities they take turns deciding on, and a few other activities that they are doing together.

Building FORDitude

FORDitude came into existence as a daily action program, which I developed as the result of over a decade of lived experience and education in recovery from mental health and substance abuse issues. I have read hundreds of related books in my own recovery journey and have sourced and borrowed, with credit given, from a plethora of different areas and avenues. I have been influenced greatly by the foundational texts of AA and the Hazelden collections and works by experts such as Gabor Mate, Brene Brown, Melody Beattie, Louise Hay, Andrew Weil, Joseph Murphy, and Byron Katie, among countless others. I have attended many workshops and seminars over the last twenty plus years, as well, ranging in topics related to my career in human resources and the financial sector to my more recent personal work in recovery from substance abuse and BPD. I have learned immeasurable lessons from years of DBT and cognitive behavioral therapy (CBT) sessions, twelve-step meetings and step work, service work, volunteering, and treasured conversations with many wise souls over the years, both formally and non-formally educated.

Fortitude, according to the Merriam Webster Dictionary, is defined as follows: The strength of mind that enables a person to encounter danger and bear pain or adversity with courage. To me, this definition implies possessing two key characteristics: strength and resilience. From my experience with BPD, these were two characteristics I lacked. Not having these characteristics was a real hindrance to coping with the struggles of both daily life and managing my BPD. The ultimate goal of this program is to help you truly feel and embody these qualities. Backed by the skills and knowledge outlined in this book, I want to help you to know you have the strength to create positive change in your life, overcome the barriers you feel and face as a result of your BPD, and build fortitude in your daily life. This is possible by understanding the reasons behind the steps of the program and practicing them daily.

Step 1: Foundations of FORDitude

In the first step of FORDitude, I discuss the power of vulnerability, as coined by Brene Brown in her book Daring Greatly. This way of thinking was very influential in building the FORDitude program, even before I realized I was developing it.

Next, I explain the enormous benefits of viewing yourself as the ultimate project and of utilizing project management strategies to manage important aspects of your life. This is the most effective way to ensure your personal success.

You will learn to set realistic goals and timeframes in order to assist you with your ongoing life management. You will also learn how to do your own healing through effective time management, allowing you to focus on what is required to be able to perform to your highest good and provide for your body, mind, and spirit. In order to do this, I will show you how to organize your necessary tasks into steps which are actionable and accountable. Using the tool/table that I will share with you, I will show you how to layout the day ahead and organize and sort out the laundry list of stuff to clear from your mind before sleep.

I will also go over why it is so important to ensure that you are consuming the appropriate amount of water daily and how to recognize signs of dehydration. Breathwork will be touched on here as well.

Step 2: Optimize Your Mind and Spirit

In this step, I discuss the importance of beginning each day with positive intentions and reading daily meditations, like Melody Beattie's "Language of Letting Go", as well as mirror work with positive affirmations.

I will walk you through the importance of believing you can restart or reset your day anytime you want – feel free to hit the reset button and begin again with new intentions. Yesterday is gone, tomorrow hasn't happened yet and today is a gift, which is why we call it the present. It is what we have, not all we have, and the key is to make the most of every day and not waste a precious moment of it looking backwards or forwards.

You can do anything for one day but having to think about doing it for the rest of your life can become too daunting a thought. Therefore, it is so important to live by the philosophy of "one day at a time".

Step 3: Reclaiming Your Resilience

In this step, you will learn about what resilience is and if you have to be born with it or if you can learn it. You will learn the qualities of resilience and examples of how important they are day in and day out. You will also learn where thinking traps come from, why you may fall into them without even knowing they are there in the first place, and what, if anything, can you do to avoid them in the future.

We will explore other common issues you may be challenged with concerning limiting beliefs and unconscious thinking that you can become aware of and change once you become aware, such as iceberg beliefs.

Step 4: Determine the Truth of the Matter

In this step, you will learn about cooccurring disorders, addiction, and the definition and cause of addiction. I will introduce you to Canadian physician and four-time bestselling author, Dr. Gabor Mate and his work in addiction and trauma, which has been instrumental to my personal recovery journey.

I will shed light on the stories we tell ourselves, which are full of negative self-talk, and what you can do to interrupt the inner dialogue that has been taking place in your head for a long time and replace it with a new one that is more suitable for you today.

I will also provide you with the definition for addiction and cooccurring disorders, explore causes of addiction and what it may mean for society to better understand, and discuss dependency in childhood and shame-based family systems that can contribute to your early adverse issues.

Step 5: Integrated Healing Approaches

In this step, I will talk about several creative healing options to explore. The first thing to ensure is that you are getting enough sleep and that you are working on your conscious breathing as both are extremely important to your day-to-day performance.

I will explore various art forms, like music and painting, and different forms of exercise, like yoga and qi gong. Next, I will get into the many benefits of imagery and visualization and provide for you examples of each. Lastly, let's look at how important and helpful it is to establish a routine of expressive writing and journaling, including a daily gratitude exercise which will enable you to effectively deal with past issues that may still be causing you great challenges in your heart and mind.

Step 6: Therapeutic Approaches (DBT & CBT)

In this step, I will discuss with you the avenues to pursue on your way to remission and recovery from BPD, which include both Dialectic Behavioural Therapy (DBT) and Cognitive Behavioural Therapy (CBT) with a focus on mindfulness.

Step 7: Universal Power and Connection to Recovery Supports

In this step, I will extend an Invitation to connect to "Source" of your understanding and choosing – be it the Universe, God (Good Orderly Direction) or Goddess, Creator, Mother Nature, "That Which Pulls You Through", or any power greater than yourself, as this a crucial piece that has been missing in Western medicine and the triangle of mind, body and spirit.

I will introduce the basics of Buddha while emphasizing that spirituality, for me, has been the single best decision in helping me turn my life around.

I will discuss healthy connections, the value of pets and the unconditional love they bring into our lives, Buddhism as a form of more structured spirituality, several types of prayers, recovery supports, including online recovery groups, and the benefit of coaching and AA meetings.

Step 8: Depend on Yourself

In this step, I will share a story from my early days of recovery, and a lesson that enough is enough in learning boundaries.

I will discuss how to understand the need and benefit of self-care, as well, understanding what codependency is and what boundaries are. You will also learn about the role of appropriate anger and how and why you will likely need to look at the key relationships in your life and whether you want to make any necessary changes.

Lastly, I will outline the benefits of reducing/eliminating gluten and white sugar from your system and the cost to your physical and mental health if you don't – because "you don't know what you don't know."

Step 9: Elevate Yourself

Obstacles

All the obstacles are surmountable if you want it bad enough and want your life to change. But remember, life doesn't get better by chance – but by change!

I won't pretend that this is a cake walk because it is not. It is your life that we are talking about, so it is worth it and worth the time and the investment. There are no shortcuts in life or to any place worth going, but the journey, and the work, is so incredibly worth it. When you get to the place where the work and practice has paid off and you can see and notice it in your actions and your relationships – you will be blown away!

Chapter 12 Coping With People With Borderline Personality Disorder

Borderline Personality Disorder is characterized by instability of self-image, emotions, and interpersonal relationships. They are also impulsive and they tend to commit self-injurious behavior. Thus, there is a need for proper communication and treatment for people with borderline personality disorder.

The first thing to consider when talking to someone with borderline personality disorder is to understand the disorder. One must be informed about it, and must have an overview about its symptoms, causes, and treatment. It is essential for us to understand what they are going through because there would be instances wherein they would have episodes in which they would have an outburst of emotions and could cause harm to people close to the person with borderline personality disorder; even to themselves. You should find time to learn the symptoms and nature of borderline personality disorder to fully motivate yourself to help your loved ones with borderline personality disorder. Here are some of the ways to cope with people with Borderline Personality Disorder:

Be realistic. We do not have the power to change a person with borderline personality disorder. We just have to communicate with them in a way that they will not feel threatened because this could inflict suicidal thoughts. One should know that even if a person with borderline personality disorder has emotional vulnerabilities, they still possess strengths such as knowledge and creativity. You should help people with borderline personality disorder by slowing down their plans in engaging in different activities or setting up small goals for them after their treatment. For instance, when an individual stopped in school because of the occurrence of the disorder, he can take up just a course or two and add another one on the next semester so that there would be a gradual transition and would lessen the possibility of relapsing. You should help them take one step at a time.

Be consistent. When you promise to do something to an individual with borderline personality disorder, be man enough and fulfil it. Do not say things that you cannot otherwise do. This will only trigger negative emotions toward you, which may cause him to exemplify impulsive behaviour. It will not be easy to handle them when they are disappointed because they would have an emotional breakdown or outburst. If you think you would not be able to fulfil it, then do not tell them because there is a need for you to establish a certain rate of trust.

Leave them if necessary. When they are already experiencing physical threat, verbal or emotional abuse, then you do not need to tolerate it. You should remember to also take care of yourself. But you should also call for professional assistance because this can also inflict danger to them. Although people with borderline personality disorder only want love and affection, there will be times wherein they will demand for too much, that one can no longer provide. Because of this, they get disappointed and they exhibit risky and dangerous behaviour. Do not let them hurt you as they please. If you tolerate them, they will not learn and they will only do it again and again. Make sure that you help them recover in the proper way.

Encourage responsibility. Knowing that someone you love or someone close to you has Borderline personality disorder does not mean that you need to be the one responsible because you are not their rescuer. You are not the person who can change them but only themselves. When they do something reckless, do not deal with it. If they stole something, do not bail them. When they smash things, do not replace them. They need to be thought to take care for themselves because if not, they will not have the motivation to change. Help them by making them realize that they are the ones responsible for the actions they make. Through this, they will know whether a particular action should be repeated or not. It will help them realize the wrong things that they have done.

Simplify things. When you are communicating with a person with borderline personality disorder, you should make sure that every detail you say would not give them any misinterpretations because they will not be able to manage their emotions; especially when it is about a sensitive issue. Make everything you say direct, simple and short for them to really understand the situation. When they misinterpreted something, or has misunderstood what you have said, they may feel offended even if that is not really your point. They will not understand you if you say that you do not mean that particular thing because they have the mindset that they are bad. Avoid these things to happen by making sure that you are simple, clear, and understandable in your words.

Be honest. People with borderline personality disorder do not realize the effect of their actions to themselves and to other people. Do not tell them that they are being treated unfairly unless it is completely true. Tell them honest feedbacks. For instance, when your loved one failed a course in his university, "I know how it feels to fail a course" rather than agreeing that it is all because of his awful professor in the university. This would help them lessen the burden they are feeling because they know that there is someone who can understand them. Also, telling lies to make them feel better will only hurt them in the long run. Although you have rescued them from a moment of rage, things will only get worse when they finally find out that you have been lying. They will even think to themselves that they can trust nobody and they are better off with themselves alone.

Remember that the person is separate from the behavior. When you are in the situation that the person with borderline personality disorder elicits violent and unnecessary behavior, it is the behavior you dislike and not the person. You should make it clear to yourself because if not, you would have a hard time communicating with them and you will not be able to give reinforcements to the particular behavior. Understand that they are behaving in such ways and manners because they are suffering from the disorder. Without that condition, they would not have otherwise behaved in that way. This is the reason why being informed about Borderline Personality Disorder is important because it helps you understand the person for who he is, without taking his actions too personal.

Do not trigger any argument. Remember that the feelings of a person with borderline personality disorder are very fragile that it is hard for them to control it. There would be instances when they would misinterpret something you told them and would cause an argument. When you explain your intentions, emotions escalate. When you try to compliment them, they would think that you are just trying to patronize them. Being the person that can understand the situation better, do your best to control your emotions and keep your sanity even though you feel that you are defeated and frustrated because of their behaviour. Reacting desperately or angrily to explain your point would just make the problem worst. Remember that you are the one who is supposed to cope with them because you are the one who has the capability to think better before doing anything. Make sure that at all times, you keep in mind that their condition is hindering them from acting normally. Do not argue with them and scold them for their behaviour because they will only feel worse.

Proper timing. There is always a good time for everything; especially when you are trying to open up certain subject to a person with borderline personality disorder. When they seem like having a bad time or are experiencing something bad, it makes them vulnerable and could not handle any negative situations. You should postpone that conversation and wait for the person to be okay. Confronting him while he is still having difficulties managing her thoughts and emotions will only heat up the moment. This may lead to arguments that could make him elicit impulsive and risky behaviour. Be the one to adjust to his conditions by holding within you whatever it is that you want to tell them until they finally feel better.

Borderline Personality Disorder Treatment

Treatment for Borderline Personality Disorder varies from person to person. Experts suggest that there are people whose Borderline Personality Disorder is easier to be treated than others. This is because people with this condition do not experience the same exact situations. Some symptoms such as anger and self-injury are easier to be addressed than symptoms such as fear and instability in relationships. Because of these variations, there are also different ways to treat Borderline Personality Disorder depending on the situation experienced by the person.

This chapter provides you with an overview of the different ways to treat Borderline Personality Disorder. It outlines a number of treatments that most experts refer to their patients. Through this chapter, you will be able to identify what kind of treatment suits your condition. The treatments for Borderline Personality Disorder are as follow:

Dialectical Behavior Therapy

Dialectical Behavior Therapy is a therapy used to change a person's harmful patterns of behaviour such as self-injury and suicidal thoughts. It focuses on the process of identifying the factors that trigger one's harmful behaviour, as well as identifying the proper measures that can be undertaken to cope with these factors. Dialectical Behavior Therapy is centered upon the concepts of mindful awareness, acceptance, and distress tolerance. According to experts, Dialectical Behavior Therapy has never failed to treat Borderline Personality Disorder among many people. This kind of therapy has four modules namely: distress tolerance, acceptance, mindful awareness and interpersonal effectiveness. Mindfulness is derived from Buddhist practice, in which a person is taught skills necessary to pay attention to his thoughts and actions by living the moment with perspective. Distress tolerance is a kind of treatment that is focused on overcoming distressing circumstances and events such as death, heartbreak, serious illnesses, and traumatic events. Emotion regulation or acceptance is a way of regulating one's emotions by obtaining particular skills such as identifying and labelling emotions, identifying obstacles to changing emotions, reducing vulnerability to emotion mind, and a lot more. Finally, interpersonal effectiveness teaches interpersonal response patterns such as strategies for saying no, asking for one's needs, and dealing with interpersonal conflict.

Mentalization-based Therapy

Mentalization-based Therapy is one of the many forms of psychodynamic psychotherapy in which a person is taught to separate his thoughts and behaviour from those of other people through the process of mentalization. It focuses on how one's thoughts and actions are associated with mental states, with the aim of helping a person recognize their effects. Mentalization-based Therapy has four main goals namely: increased affect regulation, better behavioural control, ability to accomplish life goals, and better relationships. It focuses on recovering mentalization skills by emphasizing how the present is influenced by past events. For two times in a week, a person with Borderline Personality Disorder undergoes mentalization-based therapy with alternating sessions between individual treatment and group therapy.

Cognitive Behavioral Therapy

Cognitive Behavioral Therapy is a present-oriented psychotherapy directed toward fixing inappropriate thinking and behaviour through structured and short-term processes. It combines the strategies used in behavioural therapy and cognitive therapy. Most patients of cognitive behavioural therapy are those who undergo depression and anxiety. It is focused on identifying the problems and providing necessary actions to solve them. It has four methods namely: therapist, reading self-help materials, computerized or internet-delivered, and group educational course. The first methods is one in which the patient is made to undergo sessions of face-to-face with a therapist for a particular period of time. Reading self-help materials, as the name suggests, is said to be effective for some people with Borderline Personality Disorder. Computerized or internet-delivered cognitive behavioural therapy is one in which there is a indirect contact between the patient and the therapist because the therapy is carried out online instead of face-to-face. Finally, participation in group activities and discussions is also said to be effective.

Schema-focused Therapy

Schema-focused therapy is a kind of therapy focused on four main theoretical concepts namely: schema, modes, coping styles, and basic emotional needs. Schema, according to cognitive psychology, is an organized pattern of behaviour and thought. In schema-focused therapy, it refers to life patterns of emotion, perception, and physical sensation that are self-defeating. Coping styles are the way in which a person responds to schema. Modes are mind states responsible for clustering schemas and coping styles. Not meeting one's basic emotional needs is said to be the cause of the development of schema, modes, and coping styles. There are different techniques used in schema-focused therapy namely: limited reparenting, schema diary, flash cards, imagery and chair work.

Transference-focused Psychotherapy

Transference focused psychotherapy is a process in which the treatment is focused on the unreconciled and contradictory perception of a person about himself and other people. It provides necessary skills for overcoming these distorted perceptions, which affects his relationships with others. Of all the other therapies, transference focused psychotherapy is the only one believed to have changed the way people with borderline personality disorder think about themselves and other people. Transference focused psychotherapy is focused towards reducing suicidal thoughts and behaviour and self-injury. Other goals include increased affect regulation, better behavioural control, ability to pursue goals, and more gratifying relationships. Transference focused psychotherapy has three steps namely: diagnosis description, diagnosis elaboration, and integration.

Now that you know some of the therapies used to treat Borderline Personality Disorder, it is important that you undergo such therapies upon being diagnosed with this condition. This is to avoid further serious risks and complications that might arise from the disorder.

Chapter 13 Alternative Treatments For Borderline Personality Disorder

Because medications are known to cause unpleasant side effects, many people turn to alternative treatments such as herbal remedies and supplements. Herbal remedies are natural treatments that can be just as effective as traditional medication, only less expensive. Supplements contain ingredients that may reduce symptoms of borderline personality disorder.

What Herbal Remedies are Ideal for Treating Borderline Personality Disorder?

The following are the most recommended herbs that you can use to reduce symptoms of borderline personality disorder. However, before you use any of these herbal remedies, see to it that you consult your doctor. Your doctor may not allow you to use such remedies if you have any allergic reactions or are taking other medications that may interfere with the effectiveness of the treatment.

Yerba Mate

Yerba mate was originally found in Argentina. It is commonly used as a natural mood stabilizer, anti-anxiety treatment, and antidepressant. Young children even receive yerba mate to regulate their mood swings. According to the author John Lust, this herb is also a good stimulant that can improve mood, provide relief from fatigue, and stimulate mental energy.

Kava Kava

Kava kava is ideal for fighting against insomnia, anxiety and fatigue. The National Center for Complementary and Alternative Medicine states that this herb is effective for anxiety disorders, and may work as an alternative for benzodiazepines and tricyclics.

If you are worried that this herb may interfere with your mental alertness, worry no more. However, note that even though kava kava does not interfere with mental health, it may be harmful to the liver. Many health professionals do not recommend the use of kava kava for more than three months. Likewise, they do not recommend it if you are also taking psychotropic drugs.

Valerian Root

This herb is widely popular all over the world due to its healing properties. In fact, it has been labeled as Grandmother Earth's Valium. Many people use the valerian root as a nerve tonic. They also use it to treat a variety of health conditions, such as depression, anxiety, and insomnia.

The valerian is also useful for relieving pain, strain, and tension. It also contains properties that can be beneficial to your brain and nervous system. Then again, this herb is not ideal to be taken with sleeping drugs. If you take it with a sleeping pill, it may interfere with the effectiveness of the pill.

In addition, this herb may cause hallucinations. If you have been diagnosed with borderline personality disorder, you should take the valerian root in low dosages only. You may also put it in your tea. Just make sure that you allot about a two to three week break period.

Chamomile

Chamomile has soothing properties that can improve your mood. According to a clinical study that involved people with anxiety disorders, chamomile is effective in relieving symptoms of such disorders. Moreover, it has been found that chamomile contains chemicals that can naturally treat anxiety without producing unpleasant side effects. A cup of chamomile tea is enough to keep you calm and relaxed.

St. John's Wort

St. John's Wort contains properties that can help your body absorb serotonin better. It also increases the levels of serotonin in your body. St. John's Wort is widely known for its effectiveness in reducing symptoms of numerous mental disorders as well as improving mood.

According to studies, this herb can be just as effective as traditional medications and antidepressants. If you want your symptoms of borderline personality disorder, depression or anxiety to be reduced, you can try using St. John's Wort. However, you should keep in mind that this herb is not advisable to be taken with supplements, SSRIs, and MAOIs, because it might alter their effectiveness.

What Supplements can you Use to Treat Borderline Personality Disorder?

Aside from herbal remedies, you can also use supplements to reduce your symptoms of borderline personality disorder. The following are some of the recommended supplements that you can try:

SAM-e or S-Adenosyl L-Methionine

This supplement is an amino acid that you can find inside your body. It helps produce mood-enhancing neurotransmitters, including serotonin and dopamine. A lot of studies and clinical trials show that this supplement can significantly reduce symptoms of depression. It was also found that you could be in a bad mood if there are not sufficient amounts of SAM-e in your body.

Nevertheless, if you have just begun using this supplement, you should take it in low dosages. You can increase the dosage gradually when your body gets used to the supplement. It is never ideal to take SAM-e in very high dosages as it can increase your risk of manic episodes and insomnia. You can take this supplement on an empty stomach and along with B vitamins.

5-HTP or 5-Hydroxytryptophan

5-HTP is similar to SAM-e in the way that both of them are naturally present in your body. This supplement works by regulating and boosting your serotonin production. It helps alleviate feelings of anxiety and depression. In addition, it helps your system avoid sleep problems, such as insomnia.

Taking 5-HTP before going to bed is ideal because it can help you sleep better. Then again, if you have just begun using this supplement, you should not use more than fifty milligrams. Over time, however, you can increase your dosage to about one hundred milligrams.

DHA or Docosahexaenoic Acid

DHA is an omega-3 fatty acid that you can find in cold-water fish oils. Researchers have found that DHA and lithium have similar properties, but DHA does not have the side effects that lithium has. You can take DHA capsules to improve your borderline personality disorder.

See to it that you read the labels, so you will know if the supplement contains high levels of EPA and low levels of DHA. Experts recommend that people with borderline personality disorder take one hundred or two hundred milligrams of DHA on a daily basis.

Conclusion

Dealing with the facts about borderline personality disorder is not something that anyone wants to deal with. It can be hard on everyone who is involved. The person who is going through this disorder is acting out and behaving in a way that they think they should because this is the only think that they know how to do. On the other hand, the behavior is not going to make any sense to the family and friends who are close to this person because they are the ones who are getting hurt in the process. Feelings can be wounded on either side, but after looking through this guidebook, it is easier to see why the person with this disorder is acting out in the way that they have been for so many years.

This is a complicated disorder and not one that should be taken lightly. The person who has been going through this disorder is going to need all of the help and support that they can get in order to get to a full recovery. It is not an easy process since many of the chemicals and thoughts that are in their own brain are the ones who are influencing the behavior that is there. But treatment is the only way to get them the help that they need to feel better and get back to their normal life with their friends and family.

The friends and family can work together with the person with the borderline personality disorder by offering to be supportive and be there when they are going through therapy. They can also work to get some of their own therapy to ensure that they are doing just fine in the process as well. This is not easy for either, but placing the blame on your loved one is just going to make the whole thing a lot worse to deal with. Being together is the best way for everyone to get through it.

Understanding what is going on with this disorder is often the first step. Most of the families who find out that a loved one has this personality disorder will often become more upset or mad at the person than they were before the diagnosis. This is often due to the fact that they do not understand the disorder and they assume that the person is lying to them, hiding something, or that nothing is actually wrong with them. Not only is the family guilty of this, but the person with the disorder may be feeling the same way which is why they may be so against getting the help they need.

This guidebook is meant to give much of the information that those with the disorder as well as their family members and friends are going to need to make it through this hard time. The person is often trying to get through something troubling that occurred in their childhood and this is not as easy as some may think. It takes a long time, perhaps years or more, to get it figured out, but with the right understanding and support, they are going to make it through just fine. In fact, the majority of those who get the treatment they need and stick with it are able to return to a normal life with their family and friends and they will not have a relapse ever after they are done.

Use this guidebook to get started on your understanding of this disorder. There is a lot to it and sometimes it is easy to get borderline personality disorder mixed up with one of the other disorders that are out there. This guidebook worked to try and get some of the misconceptions straightened out so that it is easier to understand what is going on and how the sufferer can be helped the most. If you or someone you know is going through this disorder, it is best to get them the help that they need right away. Using this guidebook is one of the best ways possible to help them out and get them back to the life that they deserve.

Printed in Great Britain
by Amazon